BENDABLE BUT UNBREAKABLE

BENDABLE
BUT
UNBREAKABLE

Arnikia Robinson

This is a work of nonfiction. Although some names and events have been changed, this book is based on the real life of Arnikia Robinson.

Master Publisher: Remember To ThinkPink Publications©

PO Box 10414, Killeen, TX 76547

DEDICATION

For my children and my grandchildren;

Cree, Vonte, Sammie, Lee, and Ar'Nyjah,
Dynastee, and Josiah Lee…

And for my Mother, Father, and my Stepmother
and Stepfather.

BENDABLE BUT UNBREAKABLE

ACKNOWLEDGEMENTS

First I want to give thanks to God who is the ruler and head of my life. For it is through him that things are possible. On top of that He gave me the gifts of singing, doing hair, having a successful career and having my own cleaning business. Without him, there would be no me and so I give him praise every day for blessing me the way he does. If he decides not to do anything else for me in this lifetime, HE'S DONE ENOUGH!

Next, I want to acknowledge my children Cree, Vonte, and Sammie Lee and my grandchildren Ar'Nyjah, Dynastee, and Josiah Lee. Even though I gave them life, in return they have given me life as well. It is a pleasure having you all in my corner and loving me the way you all do. It means a lot to me to see how happy you guys are and how you all love me through it all. We have been through a lot together and I would do it all over again. Let's continue to love and support one another, without you all, my heart could no longer beat. I love you all INFINITY TIMES INFINITY!

Thirdly comes my Mother and Father, also my step mother and stepfather. Each one of you have played a part in shaping me into the woman I am today. I love each of you dearly.

A special shout out to my mother, Kathy. You have shown me the positive things in life and how to call on God and be a great mother. I look at you a role model; I study your footsteps and try to copy them exactly how you do it. Mothers are the first nurturers and teachers of their children, so than you for teaching me and loving me unconditionally. I appreciate all of your prayers. I appreciate you making me decide a long time ago if I was going to be a mother or let the streets take me under. Giving me that ultimatum gave me the best gift I'd ever been given, it was the benefits of motherhood. Also, thank you for looking out for the wellbeing of me and my children as well.

I want to also say thank you to my siblings, my nieces, and my nephews. I love you guys to death. Tammy and Ashunte, we've been through some things but we've never let them break us because our priority has always been to stick together as a family.

To the rest of my family and friends, thanks for all the positive, constructive criticism that may have been given to me. Nothing like having a close-knit family and close friends.

Special shout out to my Aunt Lilly for inspiring me to do my first book and for inspiring the creative area in my life.

Last but not least, I want to thank my husband and soul mate Eric for always supporting and believing in me. I love you to the moon and back.

BENDABLE BUT UNBREAKABLE

Introduction

In the beginning, life was more than fair. I couldn't have asked to be born into a better family. I was born into a God-fearing, close-knit, and caring family.

Born at Broward General Hospital in Ft. Lauderdale, Florida on August 29th,1975 to Kathy Roberson and Craig Robinson.

While growing up, my parents were both college students so I was raised by one of my mom's older sisters-my Aunt Lillie.

My Mother's family wasn't about to let her drop out of school to parent me, so they suggested she allow me to stay with family while she returned to school.

My Aunt, who was my primary caregiver, did a great job raising me. She treated me like I was one of her very own children. This didn't come as a big surprise because our family always made sure all our close kin stayed together, even if it took for one of them to raise another's child.

My Aunt Betty, another one of my Mother's sisters, took on the task of raising my mother and their other siblings since my Grandmother Genola passed away when my Mother was in the 10th grade.

Aunt Betty took on the big task of motherhood at an early age to make sure she and her siblings weren't separated.

Like I said, I couldn't have asked to born into a better family.

Chapter One

While I was growing up with family members my Mother would come and visit me often. Although she was away at college, she tried to spend as much time with her little girl as possible, and although I loved her, it didn't compare to being raised with all my aunties, uncles, and cousins.

I became so attached to my Aunt Lillie that when my Mother finished college I was told that it was time to go and stay with her and my Dad.

That didn't sit well with me at all, but of course, it didn't matter, because what my Mother said overruled anything I wanted.

Also, I now had a baby sister named Tammy whom we called "KeKe" and our parents wanted to make sure we bonded as sisters. At this time, my Father was in the Army stationed in Ft. Hood, Texas and that is where I moved.

I remember wondering why of all times and places my parents would come back to get me while living in Texas so far away from my Mother's side of the family; the only extended family I knew at the time.

The last place I wanted to be was miles away from the people I'd grown up with.

I will never forget how much I cried when we moved to Texas. It felt like everything was being ripped from right up under me. I remember thinking how unfair it was that they did this to me.

Getting used to Texas and living with my parents was definitely a work in progress. Even though I was able to go back home to Florida and spend the summers with my extended family, it was still not enough.

Every time it was time to return to Texas all hell would break loose, however no matter how many temper tantrums I threw or how many crocodile tears I shed, my Mother would not budge. Her decision for me to live in the same household with her, my Father and sister was final.

There were times Aunt Lillie would try to convince her to just let me spend the school year with her, but that didn't go in my favor either. I had to finally come to grips that my Mother's word stood firm over anyone else's.

After my Father discharged from the Army, we moved to the city of Austin in the Colony Park neighborhood.

I was happier here. Growing up in the 78724-zip code wasn't so bad after all.

There was a lot of children in the neighborhood so there was always something to do. All the children would get together and play kickball, softball, and have water balloon fights. This kept us always wanting to go outside.

One evening my Mother comes in and tells us that we were moving away from Colony Park to a different neighborhood.

I was devastated. I thought to myself, "First she takes me from Florida, now she's moving me away from all my friends!"

I wondered how she could dare do this to her child again, but she explained that she wanted to move to a bigger house, and I must admit, she deserved it.

My Mom had worked hard all her life and I was old enough to understand that she was entitled to enjoy the fruits of her labor, so I resigned to the fact that we would have to move. I just hoped that the new neighborhood would have kids and be as fun as it was in Colony Park. I began to worry if the new kids would be nice to us. To me, those were things children shouldn't have to worry about.

Chapter Two

When we moved into the new house it was like a desert scene in a movie. There were hardly ever any children in sight and there seemed to be only older people pulling up in their driveways. I wondered what my mother was thinking by moving us into a neighborhood that wasn't kid friendly, and how in the heck did she even find this place.

One day I went outside to take out the trash and ran into a boy. He was short and a little chubby with brown eyes and brown skin and a bald fade he was coming through a trail on the side of our house.

"What's your name?" he asked looking at me.

"Nicky and what's yours?" I asked.

"Christian," he answered.

As we talked, I asked him where all the children in the neighborhood were because it seemed to be very boring. Instead of answering he went into a story about how he was looking for a guy named James because he and another boy jumped on his twin brother and now he was going to fight them.

I told him I didn't know anyone named James but I agreed that it was wrong for them to jump on his twin.

I asked Christian which house he stayed in and he explained that he didn't actually live in the neighborhood but that his great aunt stayed across the street three houses up. We said our goodbyes and I told him that it was nice to meet him.

The next day I met James and his sidekick "Ant." I told him that the day before there was a guy looking for them because they jumped on his twin brother.

They denied it and I told them, "Well that's what he said!"

I described Christian to them and even showed them where his great aunt lived.

James and "Ant" informed me that Christian tells a lot of lies and that I shouldn't believe anything he said.

I probably should have listened to them but the more Christian came around, I developed a crush on him and I think I fell for him more and more each time we hung out.

For the most part, I was a good girl at heart. I made straight A's and I feared my Mother who ruled her home with an iron fist.

She made it very clear that she was our Mother first and then our friend. Her rules were her rules and they HAD to be followed.

I began to master the art of being sneaky because I didn't want any problems with Kathy! So yes, sneaky was something I became very good at.

Looking back in retrospect, I appreciate the way my mother raised us. We need to get back to that type of upbringing today as we raise our children. There are a lot of parents who want to be their children's friends and with everything going on in our world today, we can see how that's going.

Chapter Three

By the time I was in the 11th grade, I started getting a taste of the street life that my boyfriend Christian led. Although I still got good grades, I often stayed out later than I was supposed to, leaving school early, and flat out bucked the system when it came to following my Mother's rules.

My world slowly began to change. I soon learned that with misbehavior came consequences and my mother Kathy never minded slamming down her gavel. Yes, it seemed she held a court hearing each and every time I did something out of line. I had little defense and she was the judge, the jury, and most definitely, the prosecutor.

I didn't think Christian was a bad person, but it seemed as if his intentions towards me were not good ones. The fact that he was a street dude fascinated me and I couldn't leave him alone.

One thing for sure, he was absolutely a charmer. He'd swept me off my feet and although my Mother had a lot to say about our relationship, I was too far gone at this point.

On top of that, the lifestyle he led allowed him to spoil me and you couldn't pay me to leave him or move on. After all, he loved and cared for me. He only had eyes for me...or so I thought.

It wasn't long before I found out he had other females that thought the same as I did. I was shocked on one hand, but not surprised on the other. I knew he often caught the eyes of other women, but I also thought I was woman enough for him.

Along with the other females came problems. I surely was not going to take any disrespect, so this prompted me to fight which caused me to have enemies, and that was something I didn't need.

The fighting, in the beginning, was minor, but the more I fought, the more aggressive I became. One day while we were at the Highland Mall I had a bad fight and someone called the police.

We ran and made it out of the side door facing Airport Blvd towards the bus stop. Our plan was to catch the bus but Christian decided he wanted to go back and get the car that he drove us to the mall in.

As we walked back through the mall and headed through the doors where the car was parked, we noticed police surrounding the vehicle. I found out that the car was stolen. I felt like a fool! How could I have not known the vehicle was stolen?

We attempted to keep walking past nonchalantly when someone told the officers that we were the ones who had the car.

We took off running as the police screamed for us to stop and pursued us on foot.

They quickly caught me but when Christian saw this, he turned around and turned himself in so that I wouldn't go to jail by myself.

These were the types of things that kept me confused. I thought it was sweet of him to come back for me…that made me totally forget he had me in a stolen car.

None the less, that was our relationship. We had some good times, but we had a lot of drama as well.

Chapter Four

So not only did I go to jail. I had a lot of drama getting into fights with so-called friends who were running back telling my mother that Christian was not good for me because of the physical abuse.

Yes. We fought regularly. At the time, I didn't view it as domestic violence. I had always been a fighter and fighting him was of no more consequence than fighting a broad on the streets.

Win, lose or draw, I would lock heads with anyone, it didn't matter whether it was a male or female.

It was in my bloodline-my DNA to fight. My mom, uncles, aunts and even cousins were fighters. It wasn't that they started fights, but they never minded finishing them.

All the fights I had ever had whether in the streets or in school, were nothing compared to having to fight the one you loved. The one you were intimate with, whose hands were supposed to touch you tenderly and caress you lovingly.

I had run away and left home to be with Christian. I thought our relationship would be fun and exciting but a lot of those days were not fun and exciting at all.

One night, me and a girlfriend went to visit another friend at some apartments on Springdale Road. Christian was there and once again, he was ready to start a fight because I wasn't in the mood to be bothered with him, so I was pretty much ignoring him.

He started saying little slick things to try and get a response from me and when it didn't work, he started pulling on my shirt, trying to force me to respond.

Because I knew that ignoring a person would piss them off, even more, I continued to ignore him.

At some point, my beeper went off. I asked the man of the house if I could go upstairs to use her phone and she told me that I could.

When I answered the page, it was one of my high school buddies named Kevin who was calling to see what we were getting into that evening.

Christian picked up the other phone downstairs to eavesdrop on the conversation. As soon as I hung up the phone, I could hear him running up the stairs.

We ended up meeting half way on the stairs. I swung and quickly stole off on him because I knew he was coming to fight.

Anything that had to do with me and any other male friend would most definitely be a fight between Christian and me.

We were fighting hard on the stairs, going blow-for-blow when I started getting exhausted. Christian was holding me down with his weight and I exerted a lot of energy trying to get him off me and continue to swing at the same time.

Once I got him off me, I took off running down the stairs and out the front door. I heard him ask the man of the house for a gun.

Taking off full speed, I hear my friend yelling loudly, "Run Nicky! Run! He's got a gun!"

I heard loud popping sounds as the rounds of bullets went flying. Suddenly I felt a warm sensation on my ear. One of the bullets grazed my earlobe. At that point, I do through a small opening in a gate thinking I might have been shot in the head.

I sat there trying to catch my breath and hoping he wouldn't find me. I heard his footsteps approach and said a silent prayer.

Now, morning had arrived. There were drops of dew on the ground and his shoes squished as he got closer. I was scared to even turn my head.

My conscience began speaking to me loudly, telling me that I should have listened to my mother and left this clown alone a long time ago.

I heard tires nearby on the street and thought that maybe I should yell out for help. This could possibly be my last chance to get help.

I opened my mouth but not a single sound came out. I couldn't speak. I finally heard his cousin tell him to come on because he was tripping.

At that moment, I was glad I kept my mouth shut. His cousin was the one driving the car.

I was so confused. I didn't understand why I still wanted to be with hm. I had run away from home and quit school and was constantly fighting him…. yet I couldn't leave him alone.

Chapter Five

I ended up walking to one of my kinfolk's house that lived in the Thurmond Heights projects. I knew that she would never close her doors on me. That was just the type of person she was. She never closed her doors to anyone.

After being there a few days, one of my other little cousins and I were asleep. She woke us up and asked if we wanted to go down to the Planned Parenthood clinic with her.

I responded nonchalantly, "Sure, why not?"

Even though I said it like it was no big deal, it was. I had been feeling queasy and a little sick to my stomach and although my appetite was picking up, I was losing weight.

I had heard that pregnant women get morning sickness. I was too afraid to accept the fact that I might be pregnant. After all, my kinfolk had taken me in without a question, I wasn't so sure she'd be willing to take care of me *and* a baby.

We caught the number one North Lamar city bus and headed to the east side of town to the clinic on Chicon and 7th street.

All the way to the clinic I prayed for God to not let me be pregnant. I told God that I had already dropped out of school and ran away from home and that now would not be a good time to have a baby.

I felt a little better when we arrived at the clinic. I was sure that God heard my prayers.

After getting to the clinic, I went ahead and took a pregnancy test. While I was in the bathroom, I heard my cousin asking the lady at the front desk for a bag of the free condoms they gave away in those days.

We sat in the waiting room for a while when one of the nurses came out and called me to the back. I nervously followed her into one of the examination rooms.

After closing the door and suggesting I take a seat, the nurse proceeded to tell me that she had some news for me and that she wasn't sure if it would be good news or bad news, but that I was pregnant.

My heart fell in the pit of my stomach. I guess God didn't hear my prayers after all.

I sat there feeling like someone in my family had just died.

I barely heard the nurse as she told me that the due date of my baby would be March 22, 1993. She went on to explain how due dates can be a little off but that I needed to follow up with a doctor as soon as possible to that I can take iron pills and prenatal vitamins. I was already six weeks along.

I took the papers she handed me, opened the door, and quietly walked out. On the bus ride, back to the north side, my little cousin sat next to me rubbing my belly.

I looked over at her and flashed a fake smile. I didn't want to let on as to how nervous I really was.

The ride back to the north side seemed to be the shortest ride I'd ever taken. I wished that the bus would just continue to drive and drive and never stop. The entire ride back to my kinfolk's apartment I kept thinking of the three biggest mistakes of my life. One was dropping out of school. Two was running away from home. And now three, getting pregnant.

"What a perfect situation to bring a baby in the world," I thought sardonically.

Chapter Six

When we got to the apartment I laid down and fell asleep immediately. When I woke up I remember going into the kitchen to find something to eat. I wasn't hungry but I knew that I had to put something on my stomach now that I was carrying another life inside of me.

I found a can of fruit cocktail and ate that. I hadn't eaten since breakfast.

Later my kinfolk came into the apartment raising hell about someone eating her last can of fruit cocktail.

I knew then that I would have to apply for government assistance and WIC food vouchers because I needed to make sure I ate regularly. I couldn't just live for me anymore.

Another thing that worried me was I knew that eventually, I would have to tell Christian I was pregnant.

A couple more weeks went by, and although I wasn't showing, mentally, I had started changing. I had already begun to fall in love with the baby growing inside me. The thought of having someone to love me unconditionally that would never leave me appealed to me.

I just "knew" it was a girl. I kept thinking how she would be all MINE. The first thing I ever really owned except for my clothes and shoes. I would sit and daydream about playing with her and teaching her things.

I imagined how our life would be once she got here. I vowed to always keep her hair done and protect her from this crazy ass world.

Surprisingly, once I told Christian I was pregnant, he was front and center. I left my kinfolk's apartment to be with him. We were living out of motel rooms. He would go out and hustle while I stayed back at the room playing my part as the pregnant girlfriend.

I never had to do anything because Christian always paid crack addicts to steal all my necessities and clothes. He made sure we always had food to eat and a roof over our heads.

Sometimes at night he would lay in my lap, rub my stomach, and talk to the baby out loud saying, "I'm your daddy boy!"

We could never agree on whether the baby would be a boy or a girl. I couldn't wait for the doctor to reveal what sex the baby was.

One day, I don't know what came over me, but I had had enough of living from motel to motel. I wanted the comfort of my own bed. I had started missing home.

When Christian came in I mentioned that I wanted to call my Aunt Betty and asked if I could stay there with her and suggested that he call his grandmother and ask her if he could do the same. I explained that with me being pregnant the feeling of not being stable was starting to weigh me down.

I was surprised when he agreed.

When I called my Aunt Betty, she agreed without hesitation. I didn't mention that I was pregnant and I was damn sure too nervous to tell my mother. I still had the utmost respect for my mother, and although she loved me with all my flaws, I couldn't bear to tell her I was pregnant. I knew if I told Aunt Betty, she'd tell my mother so I decided to keep it a secret for the time being.

When I moved into Aunt Betty's house I immediately fell in love with the comfort and security and the feeling of being in a real home.

I had been there for a little while when one day while taking a shower, I heard my aunt walk into the connecting bedroom.

I thought nothing of it as I continued to shower. I had forgotten that I left my purse open on the bed and didn't think about the WIC cards that were sticking out of my purse.

When I got out of the shower, I overheard my Aunt Betty having a phone conversation with my mother.

"Kat, if WIC cards are what I think they are, then Nicky must be pregnant," she said into the phone.

She paused as my mom replied and then continued, "Nah, she hasn't told me anything yet. I just happened to go into the bedroom to look for something and saw the cards poking out of her purse."

I wanted to tell her that I could hear her! But I kept quiet. My heart was beating as I walked out of the bathroom because now my mom knew that I was pregnant.

I walked into the kitchen to pour myself a glass of water when my Aunt Betty yelled out that my mom wanted me to call her.

I told her that I would and immediately begun to pace the floor. I couldn't believe Aunt Betty had called my mother telling her all my business…. then again, yes, I could. My aunt and my mother were close, besides Aunt Betty was always telling something.

I picked up the living room phone and dialed my mother's work number.

"Yes ma'am, you wanted me to call you?" I asked trying to sound as normal as possible.

"Will you be at Bet's when I get off work today," my mom asked.

I told her that I would and she told me that she wanted to stop by and see me. She never once mentioned the fact that I was pregnant.

My mind began racing and my stomach knotted up. I wondered if I should just leave before she got there. I knew she was going to be fussing and cussing and yelling at me. I didn't want to hear all that but decided it would be best to stay put because I knew I had to face the music sooner or later.

I mentally kicked my own ass for not hiding the cards and carelessly leaving my purse opened. Again, I wished Aunt Betty would have let me tell my mother I was pregnant in my own way and in my own time.

Chapter Seven

All day I watched the clock. It seemed that on this day time was flying by. When five o'clock came around my heart started skipping beats and it felt hard to breathe.

I was a bad actor when it came to fighting in the streets but when it came to my mother Kathy, I was a wimp. Kathy did not play!

At six o'clock I heard my mother's car pull into the driveway. I was laying on the couch pretending to be asleep when my mother began ringing the doorbell and calling my name.

I laid there a few more seconds before she got louder. I jumped up and answered the door and braced myself for the barrage of I-told-you-so's that was sure to come.

I was shocked when my mother came in and took me into her arms.

"How are you doing Nicky," she asked with concern in her voice.

"Hi, mom. I'm fine, really." I tell her.

She took a seat and we made small talk for a while then she jumped straight to the point and asked me if I was pregnant.

I hung my head down and told her yes and told her my due date.

My mom looked at me and said, "Nicky, I want you to come home, get back in school and promise me that you will do your best to graduate with your class." She continued, "I'll help you with this baby and be there as long as you need me to be, but you have to graduate. Can you do that?"

This was music to my ears. "Yes ma'am, I can!" I said happily.

I was happy to finally be going back home with my mother in my corner. Our home was filled with love and contentment and I would have my baby in a stable environment.

When I returned home, school had just started back and my mother took me to reenroll. Because I left out the latter part of my sophmore year, my credits were scattered and I was short a few. I would have some making up to do to graduate with my senior class.

I was up for the challenge. My mother and I met with the guidance counselor and came up with a plan. I would attend regular school during the day, take classes at night, and attend some Saturday school. I wanted nothing more than to walk with graduating class and make my mother proud of me.

Although I was mentally up for the challenge, physically I was drained. My baby was very active inside my belly, and although I loved knowing she was thriving and growing, I was completely exhausted.

Every day I left school and headed straight to night school for two hours. I did this Monday through Friday in addition to having to get up early Saturday mornings and head back to class. Literally, my life only consisted of school and homework but I loved the fact that I was changing my life for my baby.

I couldn't see bringing her into the world without a high school diploma. I wanted her to grow up and look at her mother as an accomplished woman, not a dropout.

Anyway, it wasn't in my genetic makeup to fail. Both my parents were college graduates. Education was an important value to them, so failure was not an option. I made sacrifices for my baby, just as my parents had done for us.

Chapter Eight

On March 8, 1993, I welcomed my first heartbeat, Cree'Shon Packer into the world. She weighed 7lbs and 12oz and I fell in love at first sight.

I got my diploma and marched across the stage with my senior class shortly afterward with my 3 ½-month-old daughter in the arms of my mother who was cheering me on from the sideline.

I felt so proud of myself. That may not have of been a big deal to some people but for me, it was a huge accomplishment considering the hurdles I had to jump over.

I learned in that moment that in life I could do whatever I set my mind to do if I wanted it bad enough. If I couldn't do it for myself, then I needed to do it for the one person who was depending on me in life.

After high school, my life wasn't glamorous. I was always busy trying to work and provide for my daughter. I was also still very much involved with Christian.

We still had our ups and downs but I was caught up in the illusion that we were a cute little family.

Once again, I got caught up in the vicious cycle of abuse with Christian. We would have several good days that would be followed up with bad days, then back to a few more good days, and so on.

By this time, I started becoming immune to it. One of my friends, Roxy, had introduced me to her cousin Antonio. He and I immediately hit it off. Christian would still come up missing for a few days or weeks doing God knows what and during those times Antonio and I would spend a lot of time together.

Antonio was good looking with a muscular build and low faded haircut.

When Christian found out that I was talking to someone else he couldn't stand it. I didn't understand how he felt like it was cool for him to cheat on me and come up MIA whenever he wanted then want to beat me up when the shoe was on the other foot.

I really didn't see it as cheating. I saw it as payback. I wanted to show Christian that what he could do; I could do better.

The deeper my feelings became for Antonio, the more I realized that what I had with Christian was puppy love. I was falling in love with Antonio. Not only was he a good lover sexually, he was compassionate and affectionate.

I had always known Christian had two sides to him. The side that I loved and the side that was crazy. I didn't know he had another side and that the third side was much crazier than the second.

He and Antonio started getting into it over me every time they ran into each other. Although it may sound crazy, I thought it was cute to have two men fighting over me. I had never had two men fighting over me before and it made me feel overwhelmingly powerful.

Before Antonio, I had never cheated or even thought of being with anyone other than Christian, but the constant abuse, the lies, and the other women pushed me away and into Antonio's arms and left me not giving a damn about how Christian felt about it.

One night while hanging with Antonio's little cousin Shannon, we decided to steal Antonio's car and go to a neighborhood called Craigwood where Shannon's boyfriend lived. She'd heard that he was cheating on her and she wanted me to ride down and pop up on him. If she caught him with a female, she knew that I was going to back her up because we didn't play those kinds of games.

After Shannon's boyfriend wouldn't answer the door, we drove back up to 12th Street. We knew Antonio would be looking for us by now.

While we were driving, we kept seeing a car speed up on the side of us. It would speed up then slow down and then speed up again. Thinking the person must have been drunk, we kept driving.

When we got to the red light at 12th Street and Airport, the passenger in the speeding car got out and walked briskly to my door. I looked up and saw that it was Christian.

He pulled on the door handle with one hand and in the other held a pistol. Fortunately, I had already pushed down the lock on the door.

I screamed at Shannon to drive. "Go! Go! It's Christian and he has a gun!" I yelled frantically.

Shannon took off and sped through the red light. Thank God there was no traffic coming crosswise. She shrieked, "What do I do?"

"Drive this motherfucker! He's crazy!" I bellowed.

We sped through 12th street and spotted Antonio standing outside. He looked confused as we passed him up, but we couldn't stop because Christian and Breon were on our asses.

Breon, the one who was driving, had a reputation of being an expert getaway driver. He was known for eluding the police in high-speed car chases so it was relatively easy for him to keep up with us.

We heard a loud pow and the car began to skid. Christian had shot out the back tire. I turned and looked out the back window told Shannon that he had shot out the tire.

"Can you still drive?" I asked her loudly.

"I'm trying cousin n' law! Man, we should have stopped and picked up Antonio and let him handle this nigga!" she yelled.

As we drove further down 12th Street towards the highway, Christian shot out the other back tire. The car did a 360-degree turn in the middle of the street and we lurched onto the highway toward oncoming traffic. Tears started running down my face as I thought that this would be my last day alive.

Suddenly, there were police lights flashing behind us. I never thought I would be so happy to see the law.

The police pulled us over and rushed to the driver said and told Shannon she was driving down the wrong side of the road.

Shannon jumped out of the car screaming and pointing towards the black Toyota that Breon and Christian were riding in telling the police that they were chasing us and had shot out the tires.

The police yelled for her to get back in the car and to wait there, then he jumped in his patrol car in hot pursuit of Christian and Breon.

With my heart beating and my breathing erratic, I got out of the car and told Shannon I was not going to be there when the officer got back or even worse, back up came.

"What about the car?" Shannon asked worriedly.

"What about it? It's a dope fiend rental. Leave it here, it's undrivable anyway!" I yelled at her.

As we were walking briskly up the ramp towards 12th street, I explained to her that Antonio rented the car the day before from a crack addict in exchange for dope.

As we continued to walk, I saw my homegirl Toya and flagged her down for a ride. She gave us a ride back up to 12th street.

Shannon jumped out of the car. I told her that she and Antonio could finish out the night. It was all too much for me and I just wanted to go home and wrap my arms around my daughter and go to sleep.

Chapter Nine

The next morning, I awoke to the phone ringing incessantly. It was Christian. I guess the police hadn't caught him and Breon after all.

As I mentioned, that damned Breon knew how to drive a getaway car. It was as if he went to school and passed "How to Elude the Police 101" with straight A's!

I answered the phone. When I realized it was Christian I immediately hung up. He continued to call back to back for an hour. I was starting to get scared.

It was almost as if he'd forgotten that we have a child together. What did he think would happen to Cree if he killed her mother? With him being a two-time felon, there was no way a court would grant him custody.

Whenever he was mad he would say things like, "I'm going to kill you and raise our baby by myself!"

The fool acted like he wasn't even going to be in jail for murder.

I ignored his calls and his attempts to contact me for two weeks straight. I had had enough of the abuse and his ways.

One evening, Antonio and I were riding through the Georgian Manor apartments to pick up his half-brother Antwan. As we pulled into the entrance, I spotted Breon sitting at the bus stop hitting licks, selling dope to crack addicts.

As soon as Breon noticed who was in the car he took off running.

I looked over nervously at Antonio and said, "Christian must be in the area because Breon just took off running."

Antonio looked at me, irritated and said, "So what? You scared?"

I replied that I wasn't, but any fool could see that I was visibly shaking. I began taking off the jewelry Christian had bought me before we broke up. I had three herringbone necklaces and the thickest one had an Uzi gun charm that matched my gold Uzi ring.

As I explained, Christian spoiled me with the material things his lifestyle afforded him. The only drawback was that those things came with a price and I wasn't willing to pay it anymore.

Antwan jumped in the car and we turned around to exit the apartments. Coincidentally, there was only one way in and one way out, so we ended up passing back by the bus stop where we initially saw Breon.

As I knew they would be, Breon and Christian were standing at the bus stop waiting on us.

Christian flagged us down and walked towards the car. I looked over at him incredulously wondering why he would stop.

When he rolled down the window to ask what was up, Christian asked in a friendly manner, "Where y'all going?"

Antonio immediately answered, "About our business."

Christian looked over at me and asked if he could holler at me for a minute. He walked towards the passenger side of the car where I was seated. I cracked my window a couple of inches and asked him what he wanted.

"What's up with you Nicky?" Christian asked. I could tell he was getting agitated. "Where are the necklaces I bought you?"

I proceeded to tell him we were just out riding and that I'd left the necklaces at home.

By now, Antonio was getting irritated and asked Christian to step aside so that we could pull off.

Christian nodded his head and politely moved out of the way. Immediately warning bells rang in my spirit.

As we drove out I turned to look back and saw Christian's arm outstretched with a gun in his hand. Before I could say anything, he fired the gun and the front window shattered.

I immediately ducked and screamed. Broken pieces and glass shards were in my hair and lap. For some strange reason, I got pissed thinking I had just gone to the beauty shop and now I'd have to wash my hair style out.

Antonio sped through the driveway entrance and pulled into the parking lot of a nearby store.

"I'm going to have to go back and fight this nigga!" he screamed.

I wondered if Antonio realized that this fool had a gun. Didn't he see the shattered window?

Antonio jumped out of the car and began sprinting towards Christian asking him what his problem was.

Fortunately, the gun jammed as Christian kept trying to shoot at him. I was shocked at how neither of them was scared.

Antonio apparently wasn't afraid of getting shot and Christian obviously wasn't afraid of shooting him.

Antonio jumped in the backseat of the car directly behind me when we heard the sounds of sirens. It was ironic how I was starting to relish that sound whenever Christian was near. It symbolized safety.

I sat there for what seemed to be an eternity with my head down between my legs. I knew that either way this ended I would have two families mad at me, considering this was all happening because of me.

The only thing that I could think to justify this mess was that you couldn't help how deeply you fell in love with a person, or how deeply a person falls in love with you.

I had always heard love will make you do some crazy shit, and I was a living witness to that in this very moment.

As the sound of the sirens got closer, Christian snapped and put the gun to my head and said, "Bitch get out of the car."

I immediately got out and Christian half dragged me as we ran down the street. I cried as we ran knowing that I was leaving Antonio back there alone. To be honest, I didn't know if he'd been hit by a bullet or if the gun jammed every time Christian fired it.

We ended up running to a car that Christian and Breon had parked nearby.

We got in the car and surprisingly, Christian drove me to my mom's house. He instructed me not to answer the door if the police were to come by.

Once again, all I wanted was for this nightmare to be over. I wanted to hold my baby and forget about this ever happening.

Thoughts of Antonio plagued me. I couldn't believe that I had left him there, but I really didn't have a choice. Did I think Christian would pull the trigger with the gun to my head? Hell, yeah, he would have without hesitation.

He didn't hesitate to pull it when he shot out the window. That bullet could have easily hit me in the head. Christian didn't care because his motto was: "If I can't have you, nobody can."

I believed him. At this point, I realized that I was becoming trapped by my daughter's father and he was serious about his illusion of it being me and him against the world forever.

I was so deeply entrenched in this nightmare. Deeper into the abuse, the violence, the crime, and the street life. My eyes had been opened to a lifestyle I had never dreamed I'd be familiar with.

Dope dealing, stealing, and all the criminal activity that came with the street life were now a part of my life. Also, more and more women were coming for me so I started becoming the aggressor in every fight.

I began to pray and ask God to deliver me from this lifestyle. To deliver me from this man. I knew that no matter what I'd done thus far, I didn't deserve this type of life.

I guess my prayers were answered in a sense. A few days later I'd gotten a prepaid phone call from jail. It was Christian. He had felony charges for a gun and drug possession and was sentenced to eight years in prison.

Yes, he was my first love. Yes, he'd given me my first child. But he'd also exposed me to the street life and I had to let him go. I knew that letting him go completely would not be easy, but I also knew that with him behind bars I could do it. Yes, God had answered my prayers.

Chapter Ten

I am reminded of how hard my mother begged me to leave my daughter with her and go away to college after I'd graduated high school.

She wanted me to go to a campus out of the state of Texas. She even tried to bribe me by telling me she'd buy me a brand-new car off the lot, pay for my apartment off campus every year, and that she would keep my baby until I graduated.

At the time, I couldn't understand how she could expect me to leave my first-born daughter behind. I knew that my mother would take good care of her, but still, my daughter was the only thing in the world that was mine.

Later, my mother admitted that she was trying to get me away from Christian because she could already see the path he was leading me down. I began to see how mothers will do anything to make sure their children are safe and try their best to keep them from making life-altering mistakes.

I never understood the love of a mother until I became a mother myself. I still had a lot of maturing to do before I could express through my actions how much I loved my daughter.

Soon, I began to run into Antonio. I hadn't really seen him since the last altercation with Christian but we began seeing each other again.

By now, things had changed. I found myself going through things with him that I had gone through with Christian. Loves, lies, and lullabies…and let's not forget…the other women.

Although his hustle wasn't as strong as Christian's and he couldn't take care of me financially as Christian had, once again, I became immune to the dysfunction and decided to ride it out.

Antonio did give me a place to chill whenever I wanted to get away for a few weeks, so I guess that stood for something, but not much.

I started seeing hickeys on his neck. I was catching girls running out the back door as I came through the front door, and he would constantly lie about everything. Of course, like most men, he couldn't stand it when I did the same to him.

He would lie and try to convince me that the hickeys were bee stings and that the women that were caught leaving were always his customers just coming to buy dope.

Every time I would try to break up with him, he would throw a fit. I never understood why dudes always wanted their cake and eat it too….and I could never understand why I let them.

Eventually, I developed the same attitude I had with Christian, "If you can do it, I can do it better." After all, I was Nicky Robinson. And I had always gotten plenty of male attention. So now we were both playing the field.

One day I was riding the 8 Govalle city bus headed to meet Antonio at his aunt's house and I ran into a dude I'll call "Cali."

"Cali" was a different breed of man altogether and it was obvious he was not from Texas.

We held a brief conversation on the bus and exchanged phone numbers. He was brown skinned with freckles and he had a perm on his hair. He kept it brushed back.

I had never really seen a man with a perm, but I figured this was just how men in California wore their hair.

Every moment I wasn't with Antonio I would spend on the phone getting to know "Cali." It wasn't as often as I wanted because of course Antonio started sensing I was getting ready to bail, kept me under his thumb.

I began to see how different men could serve different purposes. I respected my body, so I knew that I would only be intimate with one person, but it was always good to have somebody to call and flirt with.

Every time I'd leave Antonio to go home to my mother's house, she'd tell me that "Cali" had been calling.

"Cali" and I developed a ritual of late night/early morning conversations while he was on the streets grinding. I thought I was being real slick because Antonio didn't really know that I had been involved with someone else although he swore he would always know if I had.

I felt just talking on the phone with "Cali" was innocent, it would only be a crime if I crossed the line and had sex with him. Despite my rebellion in my relationship, physically cheating with someone was something I didn't believe in.

I have always felt that if you are in a relationship with someone that should be the only person you should have sex with. There were too many diseases out there to take risks having multiple sex partners.

I was hanging out with Antonio one day and went intside to use the telephone. I snuck and called

"Cali" and asked him if he could swing through and pick me up at a corner store on Manor Road and 51st Street.

He said of course because he wanted to spend time with me, but he also wanted to know where I was at currently.

Brushing off his question I told him to just let me know how long it would take him to get to the location. He told me 15 minutes and asked again where I was at.

I told him I was in a house in the circle behind the store but that he wouldn't have to find it because I was going to be at the store. He told me he'd be in his gray Cadillac.

I went across the street to Antonio's cousin Roxy's house. Constantly looking at the clock, I still had 11 minutes before "Cali" would arrive at the store.

I guess you can say this is the day that pimping got caught slipping because he arrived in five minutes, not fifteen.

Antonio came into the house and said, "Nicky some nigga is out here looking for you."

I tried to look dumbfounded.

Antonio continued, "Yeah he kept riding in and out of the circle so I flagged him down and asked him who he was looking for. He said a girl name Nicky, so I told him that I'd bring you to him."

I sat there for a minute embarrassed and looked over at his aunt.

Antonio was mad at this point. He looked at me with serious eyes and said, "Let me tell you something. The next time you have a nigga come to my house to pick you up, I'm going to beat your ass…as a matter of fact, go on out that door if you want to," he threatened.

By this time "Cali" is blowing his horn repeatedly. I sat there looking dumbfounded. Antonio turned and walked out the back door to serve a dope fiend but I heard him tell his friend Cornell through the open window, "If Nicky comes out of that house, yell my name."

I decided to take a chance and run as soon as Antonio was out of sight. I dashed through the front door as Cornell yells to Antonio, "There goes Nicky coming out the front door!"

I kept running until I made it to "Cali's" car. I see Antonio come from the breezeway as "Cali" simultaneously reached underneath his seat and pulled out a 9-millimeter handgun.

"Do we have a problem? Who is this nigga?" "Cali" asks me.

I told him no and begged him to drive off. After driving off I could breathe. I knew that both Antonio and "Cali" were hard heads and that situation would have turned ugly quickly.

After leaving, "Cali" and I went on an actual date. We went to the movies and out to eat. I liked hanging with "Cali" because he had a swag that none of the local men had. I felt special because he let me know how much he loved spending time with me and that he counted on it.

The next morning Antonio began calling my phone. I answered and he began talking major shit, yelling and cursing in my ear. I listen quietly and finally ask, "Is that it?"

Flipping the script, I mentioned the fact that he was just now calling me this morning so he must have had some other female over last night.

I started acting like I was pissed off so that I could shift the focus off me. We began hurling accusations back and forth and finally, he hung up in my face. The fool called back immediately and I hung up the phone in his face thinking that one good turn deserved another.

I decided that I would stay home with my daughter and chill. My mind kept going back to my date the night before with "Cali" and how special he was to me. Because I was still so young-minded, any little nice thing a man did for me excited me.

The night before when we were riding, he stopped at the store and told me that he'd be right back. He came out of the store with a bouquet of flowers and a card. I had never had a guy do that before and it literally blew my mind.

I would smile every time I thought about him that day wishing he would come over that day as well. Two days had passed and I hadn't heard from him so I decided to go and see Antonio.

I remember giggling thinking to myself that whatever girl Antonio had over would have to go home now. No matter how much shit Antonio talked, I always felt like I was the one who ran the relationship.

When I went over to Antonio's surprisingly we got along so well that I ended up staying over the entire week. My sister and her boyfriend show up one day and I jumped in the car with them telling Antonio that I would be back later.

I didn't know that I would be gone all day and night. We were having so much fun. We went to the movies to see the latest movie "Menace to Society" which was so good we snuck in other showings and saw it like four times in two days.

My sister and her boyfriend stayed back at the hotel and allowed me to use their rental car to go back and check in with Antonio.

Antonio kept asking whose car I was in. I kept telling him that it was a dope fiend rental. He wasn't trying to hear that so I grabbed some of my clothes because I didn't feel like arguing. As I was preparing to drive off, Antonio jumped in front of the car with a huge brick and told me to turn off the car or he'd smash the window with the brick.

Since there were so many people out in broad daylight, I didn't think he'd do it, so I pressed my foot on the accelerator thinking he'd move out of the way. To my surprise, he threw the brick through the window and I quickly ducked.

Here I go again with a hair full of glass. I jumped out of the car and cursed him out.

He yelled that he missed me on purpose but the next time he wasn't going to miss,

All his cousins and family members were in the front yard drinking and not one of them came to tell him to chill out and calm down. It seemed as if he was putting on a show for them and they were enjoying it. Above all, he had the nerve to make me spend the night.

I guess I didn't really run the relationship.

Chapter Eleven

That night we slept on different sides of the bed. I was damn near against the wall. I wanted to make sure he knew not to touch me at all that night.

He was content with that and seemed not to want to be bothered with touching me anyway. That was the first time I really saw his mean, controlling, and hot-tempered attitude.

The next morning, I jumped up and left before he woke up. I can imagine I looked like a fool driving a car without a windshield in it.

I was praying that the laws didn't get behind me and pull me over, but I knew I had to make it back to my sister's hotel room and explain what happened.

Antonio called me for two days straight and I would have my Aunt Betty tell him that I wasn't there and that she hadn't seen me. I knew he was tripping but he should have thought about if before he clowned me in front of all those people. I still couldn't believe he had the nerve to curse me out and throw a brick damn near hitting me in the face.

A few more days had passed and I guess he was tired of being ignored, so Antonio showed up at my mom's house and rang the doorbell.

My aunt called me from the front room, "Nickyyyyy there is someone at the front door for you."

It always amused me how everyone who called my name would carry out the "y."

When I got to the door and swung it open, I came face to face with Antonio.

"What do you want?" I asked him angrily. I looked past him and noticed his cousin's Cutlass parked across the street.

"Can I talk to you for a minute?" he asked sadly.

"You're not coming in, you can talk to me right here, "I said still mad.

"I wanted to tell you that I'm sorry and I miss you. I was wondering if you would come back over to the house and spend some time with me," he said sheepishly.

I told him that he was a woman beater and that I was done. He kept denying it and asked me to quit saying that.

"I told you that I apologize," he begged.

"Do you promise not to try to ever hit me with a brick again?" I asked him not trusting him whatsoever.

"I promise," he swore solemnly.

"Will you ask your aunt to cook some nachos? I'm craving her nachos!" I said smiling.

He promised he would ask and we both bust out laughing. I decided to bring my baby so I went and got her and I a bag of clothing together to last for a couple of days.

He came in and helped me to gather Cree'Shon and our things and I yelled to my aunt that I would be back in a couple of days.

As we were driving down the highway heading to his Aunt's house he looked at me and asked had I been sleeping with anybody else.

Of course, I hadn't been, but if I had I damn sure wouldn't tell him.

Antonio and I were getting along well for those couple of days. We were playing dominoes and cards with friends and family, smoking weed, and going across the street to the swimming pool.

We were chilling one evening when someone handed me a letter from Antonio's friend Bean who wrote a long letter telling me how he had a crush on me and asked if I would be willing to sneak out and go on a date with him. I couldn't get over how shady that was. Bean was at Antonio's house damn near every day.

Intending to throw the letter in the trash outside so that Antonio wouldn't find it, I stashed it in my purse until I found an opportunity to dispose of it.

My sister went into my purse a few days later to get some gum and happened to find the letter. She decided this was going to be her ammunition for blackmail.

The next time Bean came over, my sister asked him for some money to go to the store. He told her he didn't have money to just "give her."

My sister told him that she had his letter that he'd written to me and that if he didn't give her money to go to the store she would show Antonio since he was at Antonio's house every day trying to holler at his girl.

I don't know if Bean was scared Antonio would find out or what but when we all finished playing spades that night, he asked Antonio if he could rap to him outside about something.

When they went outside I started braiding the neighbor's hair in dookie braids which were the main style of braids back then.

Twenty minutes later, Antonio walked back through the door. We make eye contact and smile at each other. I continued to braid the girl's hair when Antonio walked around and stood up over me and slapped the shit out of me. To this day, I have never been slapped that hard in my life.

My cheek slams into the girl's head hard and fast.

"What the hell you slap me for?!" I screamed at Antonio.

"You tried to holler at Bean the other day?" He asked heated.

Then my sister jumped across the table and told him not to put his hands on me because he had the whole story twisted.

By the time it registered that this nigga had actually slapped me for real, I jumped up and fought him toe-to-toe.

Even though I had fallen backward, I was still swinging and connecting. He charged at me and I kicked him in the stomach. The lady next door pulls me and my sister out of the house and pushes us into her duplex.

She called us a cab and while we waited we could hear Antonio making threats telling her she'd better send me out of her house or he was going to do something to her also. She didn't budge at all and kept me there safe until the cab arrived.

When I got back home I told myself I would never mess with him again. Of course, it was the same lie I'd always told myself.

I couldn't believe Bean told that lie on me to get the blame off himself. I couldn't believe that Antonio thought it was cool to jump on his woman. More and more I realized that he fought both men and women. To me, a man who fought women but wouldn't fight a man was considered a coward. I didn't consider him a coward because I knew he'd fight a man in an instant.

Once again, I'm in an abusive relationship cycle. I thought men were supposed to protect their women. It seemed the men of my generation had missed out on this lesson.

That night after leaving his aunt Robin's house I really started to look at the type of man I seemed to always choose.

These men would always be cheaters but couldn't stand the thought of their woman even talking to another guy. I knew that I was too beautiful to keep letting men put their hands on me and me having to defend myself. This Domestic violence shit wasn't cool at all.

Chapter Twelve

I slowly started to distance myself from Antonio and gradually decreasing the amount of time we spent together. I knew that was the best thing for me to do.

I started spending more time with my daughter, hanging out with my girlfriends, living life and just enjoyed "doing me."

One day, I received a call from an old high school friend named Vince. I knew he had been digging me since school, but I didn't think he was my type. To my surprise, he had a little gangster in him.

When he and I started kicking it, I found out who his family was. I was shocked. Here I thought he was a little schoolboy that didn't know anything about the street life. When he and I started dating I immediately became infatuated with the Crip gang. This was different for me. It was like having another family who understood you in ways your real family didn't.

Every day seemed like a party and at this point in my life, I was in party mode. I was still young, and although I had a baby, I only had one, so I felt like the world was mine. Smoking weed, drinking alcohol, and hanging out in the Lakeside hood everyday became my everyday routine.

After hanging out for a while, I was asked was I down. I thought that meant was I down to go and fight some girls, and of course, I was always ready to fight.

They were asking was I down with the Crips and was I going to join. I tell them hell yeah, and asked where the chicks we were going to fight.

No sooner had I said this did a fist from out of nowhere connect with my jaw. Without hesitation, I slid off the hood of the car and began scrapping with a girl named Rashonda. I could hear Vince in the background screaming, "I told y'all she was going to fight! I told y'all!"

In the back of my head, all I thought about was how I was going to beat this girl's ass for stealing off on me. It pissed me off, even more, to know that those niggas were in on it.

We were going blow for blow for a good ten minutes when they eventually broke up the fight. Rashonda was wiping the blood from her nose asking the guys why they let the fight go on for so long. She let them know right then and there that she wasn't jumping anybody else by herself.

I touched my lip and felt a little blood. I was ready to fight some more when everyone grabbed me and took turns welcoming me to the family. They all said things like, "Your little ass can fight!"

I was officially a Crippette (female Crip) and I was ready to put in work. Although I was born into a good family, I had gained another family. My street gang family. I felt love and acceptance, so I took it and ran with it.

I began to make all the C-que's, getting my nails done at the C-Nails nail shop (just because of the C in the name), wearing blue hair, blue bandanas, and getting Crip shirts made.

I hung out with my family every day and everywhere we went we were set-tripping. It didn't matter if it was a group of females or dudes if you were wearing red, we had beef.

One day in Lakeside, Rashonda and I was chilling outside along with my little sister KeKe. A grey-colored Cadillac came down the street flipping and driving fast. I looked at the car but didn't pay any attention to who was driving it and didn't give it a second thought.

The car came back around the corner again, this time they were going slower. I tell Rashonda to peep the car because I started getting a funny feeling. Rashonda was playing with the little Hispanic kids next door and my sister KeKe was on the porch sitting in a chair. I needed to know her location in case anything went down.

The car slowed up a bit more when it got closer to the yard we were in. The back driver's side window slowly rolled down and I saw a black-gloved hand holding a pistol aimed at us.

I heard two gunshots as Rashonda grabbed the kids and fell to the ground with them. I had already run and dove on top of my sister and we hit the ground as well.

I knew if anything happened to my sister I would never forgive myself and my mother would never let me hear the end of it. On top of everything, she was pregnant. When the car sped off, Rashonda and I searched the house for a gun.

We called up some of our boys and described the Cadillac and letting them know that the niggas in the car had done a drive-by. I was heated. I knew exactly how the car looked and I wanted revenge.

I made sure to get my sister back to Craigwood, the neighborhood her baby's daddy lived in. I needed to make sure she was safe, but she kept complaining that her back was hurting. I made her promise not to tell Mom.

Being a Crip, everywhere I went, I had to watch my back. We did some crazy things to people and those things always had a way of coming back full circle.

One day, my little sister called me in a panic and told me that she walked to the store earlier and a car pulled up on her and someone in the back seat rolled down the window with a gun. He was about to shoot her when he noticed it wasn't me.

He told her, "We thought you were your sister and you lucky that you weren't."

I questioned my sister for names and descriptions. She gave them to me without hesitation.

Later that night I drove through their neighborhood and saw them sitting outside in their yard chilling like they didn't have a care in the world. I decided to shake their world up and lit it up like the fourth of July with gunshots.

People took off running, but I kept busting. We finally skid off. Nobody fell, but at least they knew where I was coming from.

A few weeks after that, my friend Toya got shot in the head. I got up the next morning to go to Brackenridge Hospital to make sure she was ok.

Thank God, she didn't die, but the gunshot wound to her head caused her to go blind. I would have to whisper in her ear, "This is Vince's girl" to make her know who I was. She would nod her head and hug me.

Things were getting bad in the streets, yet I refused to let go of my stomping ground. I was back and forth between the East and the Northside.

I would post up in the Thurmond Heights projects and sell dope. Every time I hit a lick I would hear Young Jeezy's and Akon's song "Soul Survivor" playing in my head. The part in the song that says, "…. run the streets all day…I can sleep when I die."

At this point in my life, I kept a pistol and a blade under my tongue everywhere I went. This became my norm. I needed my weapons for my everyday life.

Money became my "eye of the tiger." I wanted it and set out to get it by selling drugs. I was also not taking shit from ANY female. I had a very rude demeanor and I went off at the drop of a hat.

Vince and I were still together and I became pregnant with my second child, this time a boy.

Chapter Thirteen

For some reason, I couldn't stand being around Vince. Just to look at him would get on my nerves. I hardly ever wanted to be around him and spent more time at his Aunt Netra's house with his cousin Sasha than with him.

Netra and Sasha insisted that I come over every weekend in case I went into labor.

One day while I was at Sasha's doctor's appointment with her, I kept feeling like I had to go to the restroom. I go into the restroom to pee and looked down at my panties to see that they were full of blood.

I pulled my clothes back up, ran into the waiting room and told Sasha that I thought I was in labor. Coincidentally, the door opened and the medical assistant called her name.

She informed the nurse that she'd have to reschedule her appointment because we had to rush to the hospital because I was in labor.

We headed straight to St. David's hospital and drove to the emergency room. I had had a lot of false calls over the past two months and had always been sent home. I wasn't about to let them send me back this time.

The doctor, along with his nurse examined me and told me that it didn't look like anything was happening right now and that they were indeed going to send me home.

I became irate and immediately begun cursing the nurse out. I told her I couldn't stand their asses; always sending people home like they didn't want to be bothered until the very last minute of someone's labor.

I knew my water had broken because there was blood everywhere and it was an insult to my intelligence for them to try and tell me otherwise. After all, there was blood down there!

The nurse, trying to calm me down, told me she would try something else and excused herself to get a slide so that she could take a culture and check it under a microscope.

She took the culture and even before looking at it under the microscope she told me that she did see traces of amniotic fluid.

After about ten minutes she told me that my water had broken after all but was, however, seeping slowly.

"I tried to tell the other nurse that," I said rolling my eyes.

The nurse left the room to go get IV's and prep me for labor. As soon as she walked out, Sasha and I burst into laughter.

"I can't stand pregnant women," Sasha said, still laughing. "Why were you hollering at the nurses like that?"

I told her it was too hot to continue carrying this little baby's self.

For two days, I was in labor with my baby boy. It seemed like it took forever for him to get here. On June 27th, we welcomed Vonte' Johnson to our family. He weighed 8lbs and 1oz.

I had what most parents wanted. The best of both worlds; a boy and a girl.

I felt like I had to go even harder because now I had two children to take care of. Vince and I were still off and on. One minute we were in love, the next minute, we couldn't stand each other. Whether we were on or off, we made sure our son did not suffer by providing everything he needed.

Sasha would keep my son a lot. For some reason, she wanted to take over the care of Vonte'. She didn't want anyone else to watch him. I, of course, saw it as the perfect situation. I had a reliable babysitter always.

One night I had just re-upped on dope and counted the rest of the money in my pocket. I got greedy and thought how nice it would be to not only have the money I had but to add to it.

I was hanging out with a few other gang members and we talked about ordering a pizza but nobody seemed to want to pay for it. We finally figured it out, order five large pizzas, and decide to go and do a robbery. After all, we were gangsters, so we did what gangsters do.

Chapter Fourteen

We were chilling at our hotel room when there was a loud knock on the door.

"Open up! Austin Police Department!' A loud voice yelled.

Everybody jumped up and scrambled around trying to get rid of dope and other evidence. The knock and screams get louder so someone finally opens the door.

The police run in with their guns drawn and makes everyone hold their hands in the air.

"Who did the robbery? Where are the pistols and the merchandise?" They questioned us aggressively.

Nobody said a word. We all remained silent.

"Everybody out!" one of the officers yelled, leading us out one by one.

While one officer held us on the balcony, a couple of others go in to search the hotel room.

"Bingo!" one of the officers yelled holding up a pistol. Luckily, the gun was all they found.

We were all on the balcony raising hell because they had handcuffed my little sister and she was complaining that the handcuffs were cutting off her circulation because they were too tight and she was pregnant.

We got told to shut up and that what we should be worried about who was going to take the gun charge because someone would be arrested for it.

My girl Rashonda whispered in my ear, "I'll take the gun charge, Nicky. I'm still a minor, so they'll only take me to juvenile detention and they'll release me to my parents in the morning."

Another officer called my mother on the phone who by now was sick of us and told them to take our asses down.

They handcuffed Rashonda and put her in the car to go to juvie and unhandcuffed the rest of us. I did receive a warning from the hotel manager and a ticket from the police officer for criminal trespassing and was told to never come back on the hotel property again.

That was my second criminal trespassing. I had been issued one a while back at the mall. I knew it wasn't a good look.

Since we had to leave the hotel with all our belongings, we called a cab.

My mom called me and told me to get my kids and bring them to her because she wanted to keep them for the weekend.

I was all for it. I had flushed my dope down the toilet during the raid and I need to get a serious hustle going so that I could make up the money I'd lost. This was a good idea. I wouldn't have to worry about my kids and could go grind hard.

I sold dope all that Friday and Saturday. When Sunday came, I called my mother and told her I was on the way to pick up my children and she simply said, "No you're not."

I wanted to know what she meant by that and where was she with my children.

My mother flat out told me that she would take me to court over her grandkids and get a restraining order against me. She told me that if I wanted to be in a gang and out there selling dope, that I wouldn't be doing it at the risk of her grandchildren.

"You had these kids Nicky," she fussed, "Either you are going to choose to be a mother or you're going to choose to be in the streets, but you're not going to put my grandkids in danger while you make up your mind."

I got mad and hung up in her face. I figured I would just let it be for the day but she was going to give my kids! As much as I tried to act like it didn't bother me, I thought about it all day.

The next morning, I called my Aunt Betty. It was Monday and I knew my mom had to work so Aunt Betty would probably be the only one she had to watch my children.

Even though my children had daycare, my mother would not allow them to go because she knew that I could easily go and pick them up. She wanted to make sure her grandkids were protected at all cost.

I called my Aunt's house.

"Aunt Betty where are my children? Are you watching them?" I asked.

"Now Nicky, I'm not in that," Aunt Betty reasoned. "I love you but I'm with my sister on this. You have to think about the well-being of your children."

"Oh…so now everybody wants to play with me about my children?" I ask angrily.

Because I felt insulted I made threats about bringing the police and getting my kids anyway.

I guess my Aunt Betty called my mother to let her know about our conversation because my phone rang and it was my mother. She was pissed. Yes, Kathy was delivering some threats of her own.

Screaming through my ear piece, the last words I heard my mother say was, "You can act like you crazy if you want to. Don't you ever forget where you got it from!"

Then she hung up in my face.

My mother had been a bad actor in her younger days and I knew she meant what she said.

Because ultimately, I respected my mother, and the rest of my elders, I decided to leave well enough alone for the time being. I knew my mother meant every word she said and I couldn't stand it if she legally took my children away.

I decided to let my kids be. After all, I could grind harder and make more money and can take care of them better…. or so I thought.

Chapter Fifteen

I came from an era where you didn't disrespect your parents or your elders. We may have talked mess behind their backs but we wouldn't dare say it to their face.

"I brought you in this world and I will take you out," was a parent's anthem back in my day.

Today, I hate to see children disrespect their parents, but even more, I hate to see parents allow it. Our mouths would have been slapped to the floor and we better dare not cry about it back in my day.

Anyways, I called my father Craig to see if he would reason with my mother and her sister regarding my children. I don't know why I thought his attitude would be any different.

He pretty much told me that my innocent face didn't make up for the fact that I had a dark side to my personality. He compared me to Dr. Jekyl and Mr. Hyde and that with him being a preacher and raising us to know right from wrong that I should know better.

I was angry and it seemed to me that everybody had jokes about who they perceived me to be. I found it ironic that my father wanted to be in preacher mode. We all knew that there were two sides to everyone.

Irritated, I hung up the phone with him and decided since the streets were my life and I was grown, I was going to continue to live my life the way I wanted to.

My family's words were resonating within my spirit and mind. Especially my mother's. I couldn't get her words out of my mind, and even worse, her voice replayed over and over in my mind.

I tried my best to continue living life on the streets, but my mother's words had a major impact on me. Because of my mother's words and her unconditional love, I penned the following poem:

MOTHER

If it wasn't for you, I wouldn't be here;

So many times, I forgot to mention

how much I love you, my dear.

There's nothing more in life

than having a great mother;

I thank the Lord above

for you and my father.

To you, I can express

the way that I feel;

Because you have been my closest friend

Throughout all my years.   ;

You could always tell

If something isn't right;

You could even feel my pain

all throughout the night.

When it's time to cry

You are the shoulder I lean on;

You always comforted me

when life would steer me wrong.

You stayed up late nights

when I was on my last leg;

Anything we wanted in life,

We didn't have to beg.

You were always there,

even when I decided to run wild;

You prayed and prayed and never turned your back
on your child.

I'm not sure what came over me, but I called my
mother and told her I had made a choice. I wanted
to be a mother.

I thank God for a god-fearing Mother and a god-
fearing Grandmother.

My mother took a stand for her child so that I
could stand for mine. She's the real MVP.

Chapter Sixteen

Going to school in the medical field was like starting a new life for me. I loved waking up every morning and looking into the beautiful eyes of my children, dressing in my scrubs, and heading off to school.

I felt like I was really making a change for the better and by the end of my education, I would be making some good money.

I'd be able to provide for my children a lot better and I'd make my parents proud. Mostly, I'd be proud of myself.

As my future started to look brighter, my self-esteem grew stronger. Months flew by and my grades in school were excellent. I also started writing poetry again. I initially started writing poetry when I was 12 years old. It helped me to deal with all the changes that had taken place in my life. Somewhere along the way, I had given it up.

As I started to write again I knew I'd reconnected with my emotional outlet and I could express my feelings and deal with life better.

At this point in life, I was pretty much on cruise control, taking life each day as it came, but enjoying the journey as well. I met several new friends at school and I learned to embrace them.

I lived in the Chalmer's housing projects and while I was attending school, I was doing quick weave, braids, and other hairstyles on the side to make extra money and make ends meet.

At the end of my school day, I would do a few heads of hair and do hair on the weekends. I never really took breaks because not only did I have to eat, I had other mouths to feed as well, and plus, I hated being broke.

I was "hungry" and I knew that I had to get it by any means necessary, but I also knew that I had to do it legally. I loved the new life I had embarked upon. The medical field had always been my passion.

Deep within I had always had a desire to help people. There was something about lending someone else a helping hand that always attracted me.

As the months flew by I continued to make good grades and had settled into a new pattern of living the good life for me and my children.

One day, my past reared its ugly head and I was caught off guard by a reality check.

My counselor walked in the classroom and signaled with one finger for me to step out.

I got up out of my seat and began walking towards her as she told my teacher I would return shortly.

"I have a phone call for you in my office," she said.

I followed her to her office praying that something wasn't wrong with my children or my family. I was hoping it was the school calling to say my child was sick or had a restroom accident.

It was nothing like I imagined or hoped for. My past had come back full circle.

I picked up the phone and said, "Hello…"

A voice on the other end responded, "This is Officer Sinaa with the Narcotics Unit. We need you to get home immediately."

I was no stranger to the Austin Police Department. They kept my picture on file with the gang unit.

I sped back to my class and gathered my things, told my teacher that I had an emergency but that I would be back the following day.

I jumped in my car and headed home. While driving, I called my mom and told her that the narcotics unit was raiding my house and that I needed her to pray for me.

My mom wanted to know why they were raiding me. I explained that it was just from my previous lifestyle and nothing current.

She told me that she would pray for me, but at some point, I need to start to pray for myself.

Those words meant a lot to me. What I realize is that our parents' prayers can only take us so far and that at some point we need to develop our own relationship with God and become responsible for our own salvation.

Next, I stopped by my son's father's job to let him know what was going on. I mention that if something happened to me that I would need for him to be responsible for helping my mother with his son.

He told me that he would and even offered to come to the house with me. I declined his offer and headed towards my apartment.

Before reaching my place, I received a call from a neighbor, Alice, who lived a few apartments down. She told me that the laws had my front and back yard surrounded and that they were also inside raiding my home.

I told her that I knew and that I was close. When I arrived the first thing I heard was my little sister arguing with the police officers. I entered through the back door and as soon as I walked in one of the officers screamed in my face, "Who are you?!?"

I looked at him angrily and said, "You tell me! You're the one who called me and told me that I needed to come home!"

I guess that angered him. He started screaming until he was hoarse and red in the face.

"Are you Nicky Robinson?" He asked angrily.

Before I could answer my sister walked in and told the police not to be yelling in her sister's face with all that hollering and spitting.

She pointed to the crying baby and told the police that the baby needs to be fed.

We walked into the kitchen and the officer asked me to have a seat at the table.

"We have pictures of you selling drugs and doing gang activity!" He said, still screaming.

I'm looking at him yelling and spitting and wondered why he was so angry. I felt that I was the one who should be angry.

My sister told me how the police came to be in the house. Initially, they knocked on the door and announced who they were and asked for me and told her they have a search warrant. My sister told them that I wasn't home but she needed to see the search warrant before she would allow them to come in.

They explained that they were waiting for the officer to get there with it as it was being signed by a judge. She told them when they get it to knock again and closed the door.

I figured by the time the officer got back with the warrant was when they decided to kick the door in, especially since my sister had been such a smart ass.

At this point, they had sugar, flour, and all sorts of white, grainy substances spread all over the kitchen floor and counters. Of course, they were presumably looking for cocaine.

They took everything out of my refrigerator, closets, and drawers. They were searching so hard there were even clothes hanging from my ceiling fan that they had tossed.

My entire apartment was in disarray. They had every intention of finding whatever it was they were looking for.

They didn't find anything. That wasn't my lifestyle anymore.

While they were searching every inch of my home, one of the female officers came up to me and told me that they didn't find anything but that they will continue to come back until they caught me.

I told her that they would be wasting their time whenever they came back just like they wasted their time today.

She slammed a paper on the table and told me to sign it at the bottom. She told me it was a paper that outlined everything they found in my apartment that they were taking that day.

The paper listed 12 gang-related pictures and 5 gang related T-shirts. It did state that no drugs were found.

I signed the paper and watched as they packed up their belongings and left.

After they were gone, I wondered how they knew what school I was attending and if they had been following me for a while.

Nonetheless, they did me a favor since I needed to pack my things anyway. I was moving at the end of the month. I couldn't wait to experience a life where I didn't have to look over my shoulder anymore. I couldn't wait to live my life just going to work and coming home to take care of my family.

Although I had jobs here and there, I didn't take them seriously. I knew that this time would be different.

Chapter Seventeen

The time until graduation was winding down and I was looking forward to it. I knew that I had to make it to see this day or I would have let down those who loved and believed in me and I would have let myself down.

Adopting the same mindset, I had when I graduated high school, I knew that failure was not an option. I'd come too far to stop.

Although school had become my priority, I still found myself missing the action of the streets. This time it was popping on 11th street which was better known as the 1100 block.

From time to time I would slide through the hood and hang out for a little while. I only did it to pass time but I made sure to keep my hands clean. I didn't want to fall victim to the streets again. I didn't want to go back to selling drugs.

During this time my friend Christel and I grew closer and became besties. We hung out often going on double dates, riding out of town, or just chilled out. This was when I happened to catch the eye of Steven, the man who would be the father of my last son.

It began as innocent flirting, then developed a crush, and then we started to hang out every now and then. This happened over a course of six months.

One night we made plans to spend the night together and this was the night that made history for us.

That night was a night like any other night that my best friend and I would hang out. She and her love interest at the time and Steven and I were all together but we decided that on this night, no one was going to be dropped off.

We had all been drinking so we were all going to go home together. Since we were heading north on the highway, we stopped by another friend's house Raynette who lived in the St. Johns neighborhood. She invited us in and let us know that she was currently drinking on a bottle of alcohol.

We knew that none of us needed another drink, but we decided to have one anyway. As we were getting ready to leave, I pull Raynette to the side and asked if she had condoms. I told her I didn't want to stop by the store since I was tipsy.

She told me she had me covered and pulled open a drawer that was filled with condoms. I laughed. That's my girl, she was forever practicing safe sex.

We get in the car and head back down the highway.

After getting in, the couples went to separate rooms. Steven and I were getting our groove on when I felt the condom break.

"Get up!" I screamed, "Hurry up!"

Puzzled he asked what was wrong.

Irritated I asked him, "So you're going to act like you didn't know the condom broke?"

I get up to run to the bathroom hoping that I could urinate out anything he deposited into me. Angrily I thought to myself that this would not be good.

When I returned to the bedroom he asked me what that was all about.

I didn't even answer him because I was so upset. I had always kept track of my ovulation because I didn't want to slip and get pregnant again. I was pissed because here I was practicing safe sex and the damn condom broke.

It was just my luck that I did end up getting pregnant by him. I didn't even want a relationship with him.

After that night, I called Christel to let her know what had happened. She assured me that everything was going to be alright because nobody got pregnant the first time they did it with each other. Because I worked in the medical field I knew that wasn't true, but I wanted so badly to believe it so that I could stop worrying about it.

Days and weeks went by. I had gotten my first job working for a Doctor's office. I was going through the inventory one day and realized we were overstocked with pap smear kits and pregnancy tests.

I decided since the office was slow that day I would play around and take a pregnancy test. The thought of the broken condom incident was in the back of my mind but I didn't seriously think I was pregnant.

After I urinated on the stick and looked at the results, my smile immediately turned into a frown. The results showed that I was pregnant. Figuring that it couldn't be right, I decided to take another one.

I went to get more tests and take the same urine sample and test it again. The second test was also positive.

"No God no! This can't be right!" I thought to myself.

I decided to try yet another one thinking that the third time would be the charm. I repeated the steps again and the results were still positive.

I started to cry and left the restroom frustrated and confused. I didn't understand why God didn't let the test come out negative. God knew that I couldn't afford another child and that I didn't even want Steven to be my baby's daddy.

The doctor that I worked for came to my desk to ask if everything was ok. I told him that I was fine just got a bit of bad news.

It wasn't *bad* news because a baby is always a blessing from God, but the timing was all wrong.

I called Christel and wept loudly as I told her that I was pregnant.

"I took three pregnancy tests. They were all positive. I can't have this baby Christel, I can't be with him," I cried.

"Why you crying?" she asked, "Shit, this is about to be *our* baby. I'll be the baby's godmother."

She asked where I was at. I told her I was still at work but about to get off because I was too emotional to stay for the rest of my shift. She told me she was about to get off work and come and pick me up.

I waited for her to come and pick me up and immediately got in the car when she arrived. She looked over at me and laughed, trying to cheer me up. She told me that it was all going to work out.

"Did you tell him you were pregnant?" she asked.

"Nope. I'm going to keep it to myself until I can't hide it anymore." I said defiantly.

She told me in no uncertain terms that Steven was her homie and that if I didn't tell him then she would. This would be his first baby and he deserved to know.

So, I looked at her and thought if she was going to be the one telling him or would it be me. After all, it was my dilemma and my place to tell him, not hers.

"Look, take me to my doctor's office on 38th ½ street. I just made a walk-in appointment." I said frustrated that she threatened to tell Steven I was pregnant.

I started crying again. She looked at me and told me to shut up. She told me that she didn't know why I was acting like I wouldn't have help with the baby.

In that moment, I realized why I loved her so much. She never sugar-coated anything. You couldn't have thin skin and hang around her because she was raw and uncut. Although she sometimes got on my nerves with her straight forwardness, I loved and appreciated her for always telling me the truth. She never told me what I wanted to hear; she told me what I needed to hear.

We pulled into the parking lot of my Family Practitioner's office and I went in to take another pregnancy test. I had to be certain. For all I knew, those tests at the office I worked at could have been a batch of bad pregnancy tests.

I knew that it was wishful thinking and it was confirmed when the doctor told me I was definitely pregnant for the third time.

My baby was due October 24, 1998. I noticed I was due a day before my sister's birthday. I decided that even though I didn't want to be pregnant that I might as well get excited about this baby.

I still didn't know how to tell Steven I was pregnant. Although earlier that day I was on that "I'm-not-telling-him-anything-shit" I knew that my bestie was right and that he deserved to know.

I knew that I wouldn't tell him until I was ready. I just didn't know when that would be.

Chapter Eighteen

When I arrived at home, I called my sister to tell her my news. She was excited to find out the baby was due so close to her birthday.

She asked me if it was by Steven and if I'd told him yet. I told her that Steven was the father but I hadn't told him yet. I explained that I wasn't for sure how to tell him because I didn't even like him romantically.

She had the same response as Christel letting me know that I had better tell him or that she would because it would be his first child and he would be thrilled.

The following day I pulled up on 1100 block and got out to walk around and chill for a moment. I saw my sister and another girl Ree whom we claim as our "play sister". They both looked at me but didn't acknowledge me as they turned and walked around the corner.

Although I thought it was strange I didn't pay it much attention and decided to go to the store across the street and buy a snack.

The next thing I knew, Steven came from around the corner. He looked at me and grinned and walked towards me. I paid the cashier for the Doritos and the soda, grabbed my change, and met Steven half the way.

He gave me a hug and asked what seemed like a million questions. They were questions like, "What you been up to?" "Do you have some news to tell me?" "Why are you so hungry?"

I stopped chewing and asked him if he wanted a chip. He said no. Then he told me that my sisters told him that I was pregnant so I might as well go ahead and tell him if I was.

Saying that Keke and Ree talked too much would have been an understatement. They couldn't wait to tell him I was pregnant which is why they headed around the corner so fast to tell him I was there.

Steven looked at me and asked, "You're not going to try and get rid of the baby, are you? This will be my first child. I will be there for you, I promise," he said solemnly.

As the months went by I started getting super excited about my baby. I wondered if it would be a boy or a girl. It really didn't matter because I already had the best of both worlds. I just wanted it to be healthy.

I did wonder how my other two children would react to having a baby brother or sister. I wondered if they would be happy or would they ignore the baby.

When I was around four months pregnant, I called Christel and asked her to take me to the doctor because I was spotting and it made me nervous. Since Christel was going to be the baby's godmother, she was more than willing to go. In fact, she wanted to be a part of every event throughout my pregnancy.

I was diagnosed with Placenta Previa which is a condition where the placenta lies low in the uterus and partially or completely covers the cervix. This may also cause the placenta to separate from the uterine wall during labor as the cervix begins to dilate during labor.

I didn't know what was going on with this. I had never had anything like this with my first two pregnancies. I did recall a few minor complications when I was pregnant with Vonte' but nothing as serious as this.

I wondered what I'd done wrong to bring on this kind of condition.

I told Christel that this had to be another boy because my daughter didn't give me any scares when I was pregnant with her.

The doctor suggested that I take it easy and warned me that if the bleeding continued, he would have to place me on bed rest.

I'm sure my "taking it easy" wasn't what he had in mind. I was still working full time, parenting full-time, and taking care of my household duties.

I found myself losing weight because of lack of appetite. Then I started bleeding again.

At 11 pm one night I rush to the emergency room only to be told that I would have to be admitted. I tried to talk my way out of being admitted by mentioning that I had two children at home that I had to care for. The hospital wasn't having it.

One night as I was asleep in my hospital room, my door opened and a visitor walked in. To my surprise, it was my old flame, "Cali".

Although we hadn't been together romantically for a long time, he was never completely out of my life. We had remained friends over the years and no matter what situation I had going on in my life, he was someone I could always call and count on.

He explained that my sister had just dropped him off. I look at the clock and asked him how did he get past the front desk after visiting hours.

He told me that he told the nurses he was the father of the baby. We both laughed. He told me that once he found out I was in the hospital there was no way he wasn't going to come and check on me.

Steven had gone to jail when I was around three months pregnant and stayed there until the end of my pregnancy. I was grateful that his mother was always there to help when I needed anything when it came to her grandson.

I had found out by this time that I was indeed having another boy. I knew it because the pregnancy reminded me of my pregnancy with Vonte'. The only difference was is that this baby boy was a lot more active in my stomach. He was getting big and didn't have much room in there to move as much.

The doctor told me that I would have the baby on October 6, 1998, by cesarean because the baby couldn't stay in there much longer as a result of the Placenta Previa.

The thought of having a C-section scared me, but I knew that I would have my mother and best friend right there beside me.

As the time came closer to have the baby, I was becoming impatient. I was ready to get this over with and meet my baby boy, the last of the Mohicans as I called him.

The morning of the delivery there were several people there to support me. My mother, my sister, my best friend, and my best friend's cousin were all there for moral support.

I needed all the support I could get and so did the staff at the hospital because I gave them the blues as they put the needle in my back to numb my body entirely.

I went from being calm to being a loud nuisance. I screamed that I couldn't breathe because I didn't see my chest moving, then I fussed about having a severe headache, and finally I begged to go home and to come back and finish this up another day.

The doctor said sternly that it was too late for that, that we were having this baby today!

My mother started reciting the 23 Psalms loudly. When you come from a praying family, they already know who to call on in times of struggle. And boy was it a struggle to me this day.

I was still irate and screaming that I couldn't breathe as they wheeled me into the OR. I was nervous and becoming more nervous by the moment. I saw my best friend and my mother following us into the room so it helped me to know that they were going to be right there. The last thing I remembered was the oxygen mask going over my face. I was out like a light.

Chapter Nineteen

As I slowly came to I could vaguely hear my mom and Christel playfully arguing about who was going to hold the baby first.

I opened my left eye slightly as Christel held my baby close to me telling me to look at how much he resembled Steven.

"He looks just like his daddy," Christel said happily.

I nodded and looked over at my mother who was smiling brightly. I passed out again. I was later awakened by the feeling of extreme nausea and realized they had already assigned me to a hospital room.

By this time everyone except for Christel's cousin Kyree had left. She had been at the hospital all day with me.

I asked her to push the call button for the nurse. When the nurse answered over the intercom I asked her what time it was, how does my baby look, and why wasn't my baby in my room. She answered the questions in one sentence in the same order and manner which I asked them.

"It's 11 pm, you were under too much anesthesia to have your baby in the room, and if I am not mistaken I think I overheard someone saying that your baby resembled his father," she chuckled.

Not the least bit amused I asked her to bring my baby to the room.

She asked if I was sure. She told me I should focus on getting rest because once I got home I would need it.

The anesthesia was definitely no joke. I had my baby at 10 am that morning but didn't get to meet him until 11 pm.

The moment Sammie Lee was placed in my arms I instantly fell in love. I was now the mother of three kids. I silently thanked God for blessing me with such beautiful, perfect children. I loved them all to the moon and back.

My love for them inspired me to write another poem:

<u>Loyalty to my Three-Piece</u>

You wouldn't have to tell me you were hurt,

I'll already feel your pain;

As a family, we'll go through so much,

Nothing to lose, but everything to gain.

I'll always be here for you until the end of this earth,

And rewind it all back to start all over again.

Unfortunately, we can't skip the ad sides;

But there are also no rules that say we can't.

Fast forward to the good times

Every now and then we'll

Pause to rest and gather ourselves;

Because once we hit play again

We'll continue to ride it out (TOGETHER)

Til' there's no wheels left.

Chapter Twenty

I continued my life's journey and things were looking up. I enjoyed my career in the medical field and I was so proud of my little family. Waking up to see the smiles of my three little angels' faces gave me the motivation, determination, and strive to keep pushing and grinding.

I had tried having a romantic relationship with Steven for the sake of our son, but the relationship had been on the rocks for a long time.

Although I wasn't in love with him, I did love him and wanted better for him. I believed that people could change if they set their minds to it. I wasn't perfect either, but for this to work, we both had to put effort into the relationship and at this point, both of us were not.

I learned that a person should never get married or involved in a serious relationship if they are not ready and truly committed to the person. It wasn't a pretty sight to play with someone else's feelings and their life. It's unfair to give so much of yourself to a person when you know in your heart that it wasn't meant to be. That ends up feeling like a waste of time.

I felt that a person could only hold on for so long and the other party cannot expect them to continue to hold on if there were no significant changes being made.

Through the good times, the bad times, the ups and the downs, we fought for a little under two decades to get it right. We did have some good days and a lot of special moments.

Most of my traveling and getting to see the world was because of being with him. Steven was also excellent with the children, he took care of household duties and was a good cook, but he lacked being a good husband in the ways I needed him to be and at the times I needed him the most.

During our relationship, the people I cared most about and held dear to my heart were still going in and out of jail.

I was tagged team by abandonment and loneliness and the depression became so bad that I felt all alone. Although my mother was still a big part of my support system, she had her own life to live.

I never complained about raising my own children because I knew that I had them and they were my responsibility but I couldn't help but feel that no one was there for us.

I was raising my children and my niece. I'd come home after working a full-time shift to cook dinner and help with homework.

I felt heartbroken. My sister was in and out of jail. Steven was too and now, even "Cali" was facing federal prison time. I started feeling like the old Xscape song: "Who Can I Run To?"

I'd always been there for everybody but wondered where everybody was when I needed them. There was nothing fun or exciting about my life at this moment.

Going to work and coming home each day was not enough excitement for me, but I knew that as a mother, it wasn't just about me anymore.

I didn't want my children to see me depressed so I began to pretend and put on a fake smile each day for their sake. This became my norm.

I smiled for the outside world but couldn't let anyone know that on the inside I was in a dark place. I found myself going backward in life.

I was still handling my business when it came to my career, but when it came to old relationships I started opening doors that were probably best left closed.

I found myself dating my ex-Antonio when he got out of prison. I guess it was something about running back to an ex whom you felt you never really got to close the chapter with. I also guess that it's something about being lonely that will make you vulnerable and susceptible to reconnecting with an old flame once you crossed their path again.

Our relationship was ok. It was basically an on and off thing with him. One day I was heading to a job interview and he came along for the ride. As we headed to the potential employer, I realized that I needed gas, so I pulled over into a nearby 7-Eleven corner store.

I pulled up to the gas pump and before I could even turn my car off we were swiftly surrounded by several police cars.

One of the officers driving an SUV blocked my car from the front and jumped out with a mask over his face. He kneeled down on one knee and with the infrared beam from the gun pointed at my chest, screamed, "Driver! Turn off the car and throw the keys out of the window! Do it now and do it slowly."

I did as I was told to do. Another officer at the back of the vehicle screamed, "Passenger! Exit the vehicle and slowly walk backward with your hands behind your head; fingers entwined to the sound of my voice!"

He looked over at me and asked what the officer said. I screamed at him and told him he heard the man and that he'd better get his ass out of the car.

Once they got him in the back of the police car they demanded that I get out of the car as well. I get out and ask them what this was about.

The officer told me that they just needed to check the trunk of my vehicle and that they may need to tow my vehicle as evidence.

I told the officer that I didn't understand what was going on and I needed a clear explanation.

The officer informed me that the passenger riding in my car was a suspect in a string of robberies. He asked me if I knew anything about the robberies.

The 7-Eleven store we were pulled over at was one of the most popular store locations so people were pulling over and watching the action from the street. Customers were also coming outside the store to see what was going on. I was embarrassed and pissed off.

The officer who had the gun pointed at me initially went to the back of my car and opened up the trunk.

I asked again what specifically were they looking for. They told me they were looking for a rifle. They soon realized I had nothing in my trunk but a few clothing items and the usual utility items that are kept in the trunk of a car.

I was worried about the job interview. Money was constantly on my mind. At this point, I was praying my life would not turn upside down.

I was about to be late for an interview with a huge company and I was becoming more agitated by the minute. When they realized there was not a rifle in the trunk, they slammed it shut and moved Antonio from one police car to another.

The officer told me that they were actually going to take him down as he was their lead suspect in the robberies. They mentioned that I could go over to the car because he wanted to speak to me briefly.

As I stand at the half-cracked window Antonio said, "I love you and I will call you when I get to the station. Never forget I will always love you."

I walked away and he called my name again and said, "Nicky remember I love you and I always will!"

If only he knew the amount of pain I was in at that moment. I knew that with the charges he was facing they were going to put him away for a long, long time.

The officer handed me back my car keys and told me I was free to go. He told me he hoped I made it to the job interview in time and to have a nice day.

I looked at him as if to say, "You're kidding, right?"

Have a good day went out the window the moment they decided to pull us over like we were Bonnie and Clyde.

I looked at my watch and noticed I still had thirty minutes to make it to the interview. I went inside, paid for the gas, pumped it, and sped off to the interview.

I did a great job at the interview but I couldn't get what happened with Antonio out of my mind.

I wished he would call right away. I had questions to ask that only he could answer. I wanted so badly for him to tell me that they arrested the wrong person.

Later that evening my phone rang. Sure enough, 512-854-0000 flashed across the screen. That was the number to the jail and I knew it by heart.

I answered the phone and automatically pressed 5 to accept the call and I finally heard him say hello once our call was connected.

He asked me what was I doing and I told him that I was waiting for him to call.

I asked him how was he doing and what was being said about the charges. I begged him to tell me that this wasn't true.

He answered some of the questions on the phone and before you know it, the 20-minute time allotment for phone calls is up.

I missed him immediately. I wanted to know more about the charges and if he committed the crime they accused him of, but he couldn't go into detail over the phone.

The third time he called I flat out asked him was he ready to tell me. He told me, "Not really but I will tell me this much. They caught Sandy and he sang like a bird on me. There is something I need you to do for me and that's all I will ask you to do."

He never said what he wanted me to do and I didn't press him, but because of that statement alone, the detectives came to my place for two weeks straight questioning me.

On one visit a female detective came with them and after being offered a seat, she got straight to the point.

"We heard your phone call with Antonio and know he told you to do this and that for him. He said to get rid of some items for him as well. Do you have those items?" she asked.

"No, I don't," I told her. "I don't have any idea of what items he or you are talking about."

The other detective jumps in and mentions the items in question.

I cut him off, "I told you I don't know what items you are talking about and I have never seen those items before."

They go on to tell me that they didn't believe I had anything to do with the robberies and it wasn't me that they were after. The suspects they believe were in custody.

"I know," I said flippantly and turned my attention to the TV as if I was watching the show that was playing.

"Well Ms. Robinson, we can keep coming back here day after day if we need to," the detective said.

"Do what you have to do," I replied, "Are we done here?"

The detective speaks again, "Yes. We're done for now. We'll be back if we have any more questions and we may even come back with a search warrant to search your home," he said in a matter of fact tone.

"That's fine. I'll be here," I said dismissing them.

The nerve of them sitting in my home questioning me about some shit that I already explained to them that I knew nothing about.

I became angry with Antonio. What was the hell wrong with him trying to get me to get rid of some items that I didn't know anything about? I know that Antonio knew how much I had going on and that I didn't have time for this. I definitely didn't have time to deal with any more damned detectives.

Chapter Twenty-One

Two days later I was up early that morning spring cleaning. I had all the windows up and all my window blinds opened.

I walked into the living room and happened to glance out the window and saw the same detectives' car pulling up once again.

I had my music blasting since that's how I liked to clean and thought to myself, "Here we go again!"

The JaRule and Charlie Baltimore song "Down Ass Chick" blasted from the speakers. As the detectives walked up to my front door, Charlie Baltimore's verse was playing, *"Now I'ma show you blood or love there's no belly you bounce from. Blow selling-dough amounts to no telling. There'll be no telling, snitches get it back. Those gats to your back for my boys. What part of the game is that, huh?"*

As the detectives got closer to the door, I replayed the part where the song said, *"There'll be no telling..."*

I heard one of the detectives say, "That must be her favorite part of the song."

I opened the door before they knocked.

"So, it's you two again," I said nonchalantly, "What do you need now?"

The female asked if I happened to remember anything. I told her that I hadn't. The male detective asked sarcastically, "So, I guess you won't mind coming down to the police station with us to write a statement saying you don't remember anything?"

I told them that I needed to call my mother first. When I got my mother on the phone, I explained to her that the detectives were wanting me to go down to the police station and make a statement stating I didn't know anything about the robberies.

My mom asked me if I was sure that I didn't have anything to do with it or have any knowledge of it. I assured her that I didn't.

When I hung up the phone, one of the detectives mentioned that they had subpoenaed my phone records and were interested to know why my phone was in my mother's name.

I told them so what, she doesn't have anything to do with it. They asked if they could speak with my mother and I told them no.

Why the hell did they want to talk to my mother? I gathered my sandals and headed towards the door.

"I'm ready. Let's go," I said in a hurry to get this over with.

As we headed down the highway towards the police department, the detective attempted to make small talk with me. I was completely silent. I didn't care to talk.

"Nicky, are you a Texan?" the detective asked.

"I'm pretty sure you know where I was born. You know everything else about me," I quipped.

The female officer chimed in, "You can loosen up you know. You're not in any trouble. We would just like for you to listen to something that we think you'd find amusing and write your statement."

I tuned them out until we arrived at the station. Once inside the building, they took me up to the third floor and sat me inside a small room with a round table.

"We'll be right back," the officer said, "Would you like something to drink?"

I declined and told them that I was just ready to get this over with. When they left, I sat alone in the room for nearly five minutes. I figured they were somewhere looking at me on camera trying to monitor my body language.

When they returned, I burst into laughter as my stomach growled loudly. I should have asked them for a bag of chips.

"Sorry to keep you waiting," the detective said as he plugged up a small recorder. "We have a recording that we'd like for you to hear."

He pressed play and I heard Antonio's voice giving directions and a list of things to do to his cousin. His cousin was apparently not pleased with being brought into this and asked Antonio why he couldn't have Nicky do it.

Antonio could be heard saying, "I only trust Nicky to a certain extent. She doesn't know anything about the money."

At that point, they paused the recording and looked at me. They could see the anger written all over my face.

One of the detectives looked at me and smirked, "Are you mad because you found out that your boyfriend doesn't trust you,"

I looked at her sardonically and replied, "No, I'm mad because it's obvious you know that I don't know anything about this and you've continuously harassed me and wasted my time."

It was true. I wasn't mad at Antonio. The same way he got me involved was the same way he released me from all involvement- by running his damned mouth on those jailhouse phones.

The male detective tried to smooth things over by saying, "Well, we will take you back to your home and we hope you understand that we were just doing our jobs. By Antonio making those statements to you, we had to follow up on every lead."

I said ok, but in the back of my mind, I knew that their plan failed. They thought I would get mad at Antonio for saying he didn't trust me and that I would just start talking or even making things up about the robberies out of spite. Sorry, but I don't romance the other team. I knew how crooked laws could be, besides, Antonio was my heart.

Three days later my phone rang. It was Antonio. Once again, I pressed 5 indicating that I would accept the collect call from the jail.

He asked me what I was doing. I told him nothing at the time, but I proceeded to tell him about the detectives and how they harassed me for weeks and finally took me to the jail to write a statement and listen to the recorded conversation of him and his cousin.

He was quiet for a moment then said that he hoped I wasn't mad at him. I told him that I wasn't but I was sure that the detectives thought I would be. We both chuckled at that.

He went on to say that he went ahead and pleaded guilty to the charges so that I and other people wouldn't be subpoenaed. He said that he couldn't bear the thought of seeing me walk into the courtroom having to testify for him knowing they would tear me to shreds to prosecute him.

"I love you too much for that," he concluded.

Finally, Antonio was sentenced. We kept in touch for a while but eventually, we faded over time. I knew that he expected me to stay down with him, and I did for a while and although I wasn't writing him as often, I still thought about him from time to time. As they say…. the beat goes on.

Chapter Twenty-Two

Life went on. I moved into a house in Pflugerville, Texas. I enjoyed my life and my children. I steadily built my career and I didn't look back. I made the move to Pflugerville because the rent prices were lower and the school district was better.

Every move I made, I made with my children in mind. I wanted to move out of Austin so that my children would get a better education and live in a better neighborhood.

Of course, they were not pleased at first, but much like it was when I was a child, they didn't have a chance to argue their point. My word was final.

They were relieved when a few of their friends' mothers had the same idea and moved to Pflugerville also. Most people were moving out of Austin and were now our neighbors in the same subdivision. My children didn't have to complain, after all, life hadn't changed as far as their friends.

I worked extra hard to make sure I kept our heads above water and to make sure my children and I had everything we needed. I never wanted to be the parent whose answer was no every time their child asked for something.

At this point, Steven was in and out of the picture, so I made sure my children didn't suffer because of that. I made sure my children wore the latest trendy clothes and had some of the things that everyone else had. I didn't want them to feel the stress of what it was like being a single parent. No child should have to feel that.

My relationship with Steven was a roller coaster ride. One minute we were up and the next we were down. That rides taught me a lot about relationships. It showed me what I wanted and what I didn't want. It taught me the difference between being a down ass chick and a dumb ass chick.

The relationship lasted longer than it should have. Over the years my love grew for him. All I wanted was for him to stay out of jail and be with us. I wanted him to stop leaving us alone by ourselves.

My children were getting older and were giving me typical teenage behavior. Although they did give me a few heartaches and headaches, they were still my pride and joy.

The challenges of motherhood came back to me full circle. Everything that I put my mother through, my oldest two children were now putting me through. I still didn't have it as bad as my mother did, so for that, I was grateful.

Most of my time was spent with my children and my best friend. My loyalty lied with my children first and foremost. Everything else had to fall in place. It was all about them.

I loved kicking it with my best friend, though. She was a loyal friend and I knew that real friends were hard to find.

I knew that I could call on her and count on her without a shadow of a doubt and she knew she could do the same with me.

They don't make friendships like that anymore! Too many women like to compete and hate on each other. They'd smile in your face and talk behind your back and can't stand to see the next woman get ahead.

One day Christel called me and told me that she'd been feeling a little sick. She'd gained a lot of weight but I knew that it wasn't just obesity that had her ill, she also had a broken heart.

She'd went through some things in life and those things had taken its toll on her. Those things took had taken its toll on me as well. This was my bestie. Anything that she went through, I went through. Any pain that she felt. I felt.

We talked plenty of times and I would tell her how I felt about her situation. She'd tell me how she felt about it too. Not only was obesity a fatal disease, depression was fatal also.

We'd been through our shares of ups and downs also, don't get me wrong, just like real friends do, not to mention, she was my youngest son Sammie's Godmother.

A few days had passed and she called me again and told me that she was still sick and ended up in the hospital. She told me that she actually died and they had to bring her back.

That didn't sit well with me at all. I was upset because she didn't call me when she went to the hospital knowing I would have been right there. I made her promise that the next time she went to the hospital she would call me.

We kept in touch often. I called her one day just to tell her how much I loved her and that if she ever needed anything to let me know.

I was very emotional on that call because I knew in my spirit that something wasn't right. She told me that she knew that I loved her and that the last thing she wanted to do was hurt me, her Godson, or my family. She again said she was going through a hard time.

We said our love you's and our goodbye's.

Shortly after our call, I called my mother in tears. I expressed to my mother my love and concern for my friend and how I wanted the best for her. My mother asked had I called and told her that personally and I assured her that I had.

My mother comforted me by saying, "Well Nicky, that's all you can do for her. You just have to continue to pray for her and let her know that you will be there if she needed you."

My mother always knew what to say to calm me down. She had a way with words that made me feel like everything was going to be ok.

A week later at 5 o'clock in the morning, my phone rang. I woke up out of my sleep and answered it. On the other end of the phone, I heard my best friend's daughter's voice.

"Nicky..." she said tearfully.

"What's wrong with your mother?" I ask sitting up.

She went on to tell me that her mother died and my heart nearly stopped. I had never experienced that kind of pain before behind a friend.

I couldn't believe it. My best friend. My ride or die. My son's Godmother. My sister from another mister was gone.

I let out a huge scream and fell to my knees. I don't remember if I ever hung up the phone or not. My daughter heard me crying and came into my bedroom to find out what was wrong.

I told her what had happened and Cree began crying also. One by one my bedroom filled with my other children, each one of them hurt to find out that Christel had gone on to be with God.

I could barely get dressed for work and my kids were slow-poking as well. I heard Sammie sadly tell his siblings, "I'm glad I got to spend the other day with my Godmother when she took me to the movies and stuff."

I headed out the door to work and I played my Marvin Sapp CD all the way to work. "Never Would Have Made It" was the song I listened to while tears streamed down my face.

I sang a couple of words to the song and found myself screaming again. I wanted to know why God had to take her? Why that one?

God knew she was like my sister. She was the only person that had never left me. Everything I went through, she went through with me. We shared everything with each other.

I made it to work, only to be sent home early. I couldn't stop crying and I was no good there.

Once I made it home I called her mother so that she could tell me exactly what had happened. I wanted to be told the details about the very last minutes of my best friend's life.

Her mother told me everything she knew. After we hung up, I cried out loud asking Christel why she had to leave me. I screamed that she promised me she would call the next time she was sick.

I cried until I was hoarse. I felt like a little girl wondering who was going to be my best friend now? Who would I be able to call at all times of the night? Who would I tell my secrets to? And who would put me in my place and tell me when I was wrong without sugar coating a thing?

We had dreams and plans as best friends. She was such a big part of my life. I sat down and did the only thing I knew to do when I was experiencing painful emotions or have something on my heart. I wrote her a poem…

<u>Christel O. Valentine</u>

Don't ever think I ever

got the chance to tell ya'

Goodbye;

As a matter of fact, I know I didn't,

You didn't want me to know and I don't know
why.

You were like another one of my sisters

Through any and everything I was by your side;

Close to you like I am my religion

So, when you were sick,

I don't know why my number wasn't dialed.

I'm still pondering over that question

Once told me that

You love me, your Godson, and my family

You didn't want us to worry.

I told you that

When two people share a bond like we do;

Your story becomes my story

Whatever it is that you're going through.

Why not call on me?

I would have went through it too.

That's something we both knew about each other.

All those times I had to call you.

So many times, you had to be in my corner

Thinking back to our last Christmas.

I remember brushing your hair, you were tired and
restless

I tried to quickly flee;

You opened your eyes saying,

"Oh, you're leaving me?"

I said

I was dipping out because you were falling asleep.

Your formed a grin and said, "No I wasn't"

I laughed and said

"Christel cut it out, you were snoring."

Friend, I even remember our last conversation and
I'm thinking too

Myself, I would have called every day up until the
last day;

When I received the phone call at 5 o'clock in the
morning

I knew something was wrong right away.

Your daughter never rung my line that early

So, my first reply was,

"Good morning, how is your mother?"

Then I let out such an enormous cry

Surprised I didn't wake the neighbors.

The news she delivered changed my life

From that moment, all the way until forever.

Who's going to be my best friend now?

Who's going to give me straight advice?

Who'll know what to do when I'm down?

To lift my spirits back high?

What friend will I trust in?

Or put as a reference on the school's emergency
contact list?

What friend will love my baby as if they were
hers?

Who's going to always answer her phone

no matter what time I call?

I came into the knowledge now

that everything has its season

You were here to show me how

True friends love unconditionally.

I'll forever hold on to our bond, and the many of
life lessons;

But most of all…

I'll forever hold on to your love and darling
friendship.

Chapter Twenty-Three

The hardest days of my life was getting over my best friend's passing. Once again, I felt that someone I held dear to me had left me. Then it was so hard to deal with the fact that I was so used to calling her and hearing her voice. Whenever I got exciting news or wanted to vent, I picked up the phone, only to hang it up once I realized she would not be picking up the other end. I was constantly reminded that she was no longer here.

I still think of her and my thoughts are always, "Rest in Heaven Baby Doll" I knew that she could see that I had kept going with my dreams and everything that I wanted to accomplish. I knew that she was proud even though a couple of years had passed by then since her death, I knew that she saw that I was rocking the thing called LIFE.

One particular day my Mother called to tell me that she was taking my daughter and my niece Ashunte to the doctor to get birth control.

I told her to call me when she got there.

A few hours later my mother called and told me that they were still at the doctor's office and had given both girls pregnancy test before they could prescribe them birth control. She went on to inform me that Cree, my daughter, was already pregnant.

"Did you know she was pregnant already Nicky?" my mother asked quite irritated.

It was my turn to be irritated, "Now mama, if I knew she was pregnant, why would I send you all the way to the doctor's office to get birth control?"

My mother responded angrily, "I was just asking, what are you getting smart for?"

"I'm not getting smart mama," I replied softening my voice. Suddenly I felt it best to just get quiet. I didn't want to argue with my mother.

"Hello? Hello? Are you still there?" she questioned.

"Yes ma'am, I'm still here."

"Are you mad?" she wanted to know.

"No mama."

"Well are you at least disappointed?" she asked.

"No, I'm not mama," I said, "Mama why do you keep asking me all these questions?"

"I'm just trying to see where your head is at Nicky," she said.

I told her that I would call her back and hung up the phone to try and figure out how I really felt. I guess I didn't know how or what I was supposed to be feeling.

I was curious as to how Cree had gotten pregnant. As far as I knew, no boys had been at my house. I called my mother back and asked her to put my daughter on the phone.

"So, you're pregnant Cree?" I asked her.

"Yes," she answered softly.

"So, what are your plans?" I immediately ask.

"I want to keep it, mama," she said quickly.

I battled with that. She was only fifteen. She hadn't finished high school yet! Then I stopped and thought back to when I was a pregnant teen. My mind was racing, my heart was beating fast, it felt like I was experiencing Deja Vu.

I told myself that I couldn't let her have the baby, but I didn't want to tell her to have an abortion either. I decided to call her Grandmother on her father's side and talk to her about it.

Deborah advised me not to try and make her have an abortion. She told me that I should trust Cree to make the best decision she could for herself.

"You're either going to support her or not," she went on to say, "You don't want her to resent you for the rest of her life if you make her have an abortion."

Then words from Genesis 1:22 from the Bible came to mind. "Be fruitful and multiply."

Although my mind was still not at ease, the song "Jesus Loves the Little Children" began playing in my head. Tears rolled down my face. I asked the Lord what was I supposed to be feeling right now knowing my baby was having a baby.

Then I heard a small voice say to me, "You were once a baby having a baby. You give her the same opportunity that your mother gave you."

Nonetheless, I sat my baby girl down and gave her the exact same speech my mother had given to me fifteen years prior when I was pregnant with her. I added a little extra information based on my own experience and told her that there may be some people who looked down on her, her family, and her friends, but I encouraged her to hold her head high and succeed.

I told her that many people will have something to say about her situation but to never forget where she came from. Never forget who you have in your corner, and that this situation didn't define her. I explained that how you *handle* the situation is what defines you. I reminded her that no matter who was against her, her mother was always for her.

From that moment, she knew that if nobody else had her back, her mother did. So, month after month, I made every doctor's visit. I even talked Cree into naming the baby after me. Loved being there with her seeing the sonograms, watching the baby grow, and feeling her kick inside. I was patiently awaiting Ar'Nyjah's arrival.

One morning about 3 am, someone tapped me on my shoulder, waking me up. I looked up to see Cree standing over me.

"Mamma, I keep peeing and my stomach is cramping," she moaned.

"Are you having contractions?" I asked, forgetting she'd never experienced having a baby.

I figured that she was maybe having Braxton Hicks so I told her to go and lay down and let me know if the cramps start coming regularly.

About five minutes later, she tapped me on my shoulder again.

"Mamma, I'm getting irritated, because the urine won't stop coming out." She said worriedly.

Her leg was shaking nervously as if she were in trouble. I looked at her thinking what the hell is she talking about she can't stop peeing?

Then it hit me. Her water had broken.

"Girl, you aren't pissing. Your water bag broke! Do you hurt? Are you in pain?" I asked as I got up and started getting dressed.

I told her to grab her bag and head to the car while I found my keys and got the doctor on the phone.

We jumped in the car and sped down the highway heading to St. David's hospital. I looked over at Cree. She was handling it like a soldier, she hadn't shed a single tear.

We made it to the hospital and just as I suspected, Cree's water had broken and baby Ar'Nyjah was on her way. The date was May 4, 2009, and one of the happiest days of my life. Ar'Nyjah was my Twinkle Twinkle Little Star, and that's where she got her nickname "Twink".

Chapter Twenty-Four

Seeing my daughter give birth gave me another new-found purpose in life. There was something about birth and newness that went hand in hand together.

I decided that I wanted to go back to school. I would stop making excuses like I had for the past ten years and just do it.

I called everyone for a family meeting. We hadn't had one in a while and it was definitely long overdue. We used to have family meetings at least twice monthly but we had slacked off with all that had been happening with Cree. Our family meetings were a time that we could air out our grievances and put everything on the table whether good, bad, or indifferent. We opened and ended our family meetings with prayer.

As we sat down, Cree, Vonte', Sammie, and I, I said prayer and began with my assessment of everything that had happened since our last meeting before I officially made my announcement.

I told them that I had applied to school to further my education and that I needed for everyone to pull together as a family. I explained that I wouldn't have the time nor the fortitude to deal with everyone's issues.

They all shook their head in understanding and each encouraged me to pursue my dream. I looked over at Steven and told him, "That means if you go back to jail, I'm not going to keep holding you down, because I've done for everybody and now it's time for me to focus on me."

"I know. I'm not going back," he responded.

I look at the rest of the children and say, "All this getting in trouble at school and having me leave to come and talk to principals and teachers has got to stop. Cree and Vonte' all the fighting ya'll do having me in court can't happen anymore." I continue looking at Sammie, "and Sammie, quite giving your teachers a nasty attitude and having to go to the principal's office all the time!"

I went on to explain that I needed a hundred percent from each of them and that although this wasn't going to be easy, I needed their support.

Everyone nodded their head in agreement and gave me their word that things would go a lot smoother than they had been.

I became more and more excited the closer it came for me to go back to school. I had signed up to pursue a Bachelor's in Social and Criminal Justice.

Our new addition to the family was getting a lot of attention and life was good for the moment.

I really enjoyed watching my grandbaby grow and go through various stages of infancy. Before long, it was time for Cree to graduate. I couldn't explain the amount of joy I had in my heart. I was so proud of her.

I was so grateful that she listened and took my advice and decided that education was the key to her future, especially when you have children.

I feel that one of the problems with today's society is that they tend to look down on pregnant teens, as if they have cursed the world for making a mistake and getting pregnant. Even though as parents we want the best for our children and would prefer them wait until marriage and career to have a baby, it's not always realistic with all the outside, negative influences the youth have today.

The best advice I can give a teen mother is to keep fighting and pushing to prove to the world and those who doubt you that you can still be successful. Having a baby doesn't mean your goals in life must end. The choices you make *after* you have your child will dictate how your life will turn out. Failure should never be an option.

Chapter Twenty-Five

Family traveled from all over to see Cree graduate. I screamed and cried louder than anyone in the audience when my daughter walked across the stage. I knew firsthand the obstacles she had to overcome.

After the graduation, we had a huge party and we had a blast. Cree received a lot of great gifts and a lot of money. Our family tradition on my mother's side was that all the aunts and uncles send a monetary gift to the graduate.

Things were looking up with my family and God was still in the blessing business. Because Cree had gotten her own place, I moved out of my house into a smaller apartment. There was no need to keep the bigger place.

My foundation shifted. I was saving money and trying to rebuild my credit. When I moved to the apartment I briefly worried about what everyone would think of me downsizing. I called my mother to have a conversation with her about it.

I told her I felt people were judging me and talking about me for moving into an apartment. People knew that I always had to have the biggest, nicest things and I didn't want anyone to think that I had fallen off.

I soon realized that no matter what you told a person, people would always assume and put their own spin on what they thought and run their mouths with the lie.

My mother told me that I had done it all and that she was so proud of everything I had accomplished. She told me that I had worked for everything I've wanted in life and that I shouldn't let anything that anyone says get me down.

I had to sit down and look at all the things I had accomplished by the age of 26. I had had a house, three cars that were paid for, my children always wore nice clothes, and welfare hadn't done a thing for me. Most of all, I had a career and it was going great.

My mother went on to tell me that anything I've had once can be gotten again.

My mother…the real MVP. She always knew what to say and how to get the message across to me in a way that would lift me up.

A month after I moved into my apartment, my mother came to visit. She complimented me on how cozy my apartment was and she mentioned that every time she visited she wanted to just go to sleep and get some good rest because of the peacefulness she felt there.

I agreed. I admitted that no matter how big my previous house was and how much room it had, I had found more peace in my two-bedroom apartment.

I was finally content with my decision; I needed the peace of mind. I realized that sometimes having more didn't necessarily make you happier. Downsizing gave me back my peace of mind.

One night I received a phone call. I looked at my caller ID and recognized the familiar number; 512-854-0000. Travis County Jail. Once again, Steven was back in jail. I knew at that moment the ride I had been on with him going in and out of jail had come to an end.

He had already missed Cree's graduation and now he was about to miss Vonte's and my niece's Ashunte's graduation as well.

I said a silent prayer thanking God that we had two more children in our family graduating. I was just as proud of them as I was when Cree graduated.

I let the call go to voicemail and turned over and went to sleep.

My Blessings

Someone asked me

It must feel good to be a single parent

Already achieving having two high school
graduates.

I replied, "It's a feeling that I couldn't explain the
world's largest ruler couldn't measure it."

When I look at all my children

and see their many accomplishments

it's an emotion that brews up within;

For as long as I live,

The peak of my love will never descend.

Someone asked me

was there a moment that I ever regretted?

Do you wish you would have waited?

I replied, "I wouldn't change a thing"

Late teen when I had my first child;

The other two followed shortly,

The Bible says, "Be fruitful and multiply"

So why regret what God gave me?

He chose the perfect three;

To be loved and cared for by me.

I might have felt somewhat alone,

But I was never by myself,

For I gave them back to God long ago,

knowing they'd be in perfect hands;

This parenting road is mighty long,

No detours, no dead-ends.

Laid a foundation very strong,

At this rest stop we called home.

Wood and nails that was my pain,

cement was my strength;

I sweated joy and peace,

securing the perimeter with bricks.

Built a chimney out of stone,

to help ventilate my stress;

used slate on the roof

for longevity, making sure it lasted.

Wooden doors for the front and back;

although expensive, I needed them,

because they were not easy to crack.

Even though they had part-time fathers,

every day I clocked in;

I remained a full-time mother,

didn't want to lose those benefits.

of watching the seed I've loved and nourished

become a successful young lady and two
gentlemen.

Chapter Twenty-Six

A few months later, my Aunt Lillie convinced me to publish the poetry I'd been writing since the age of 12 into a book.

I was hesitant at first. Now, I was a mother that was working full time and going to school full time. If it weren't for my Aunt encouragement and persistence and the help she gave me, my very first book would have never been published.

I was excited. I had so much going for me during that time in my life. My children seemed to be doing well, we all were in good health, they were graduating, and I was now an author of a book entitled "Experiences with Love".

I had to take a moment to tell the Lord thank you! He'd been so good to me and my family.

Soon, people started knowing me by name and I was getting calls to do appearances, book signings, and invited by local community groups around Austin, Texas to help reach others.

Because I loved giving back, I rarely said no to a request. I felt like I was on a natural high. I was soaking in all the good feelings from living a productive life.

I thought to myself how fortunate I was to have come from where I started and can tell others that God is able.

I knew if God did it for me…the girl whose picture hung downtown on the wall of the gang unit, the one who's house had been raided, the one who gangbanged and shot at people…he would do it for others.

One day out of the blue, I started going through issues with my oldest son. He wouldn't listen to me and he was acting up badly. My heart was aching. He didn't see anything wrong with his actions and would continually rebel. On top of that I was at the end of school, but I felt like I just couldn't go any further.

I began to pray, "Lord, you have to step in! I'm about ready to throw in the towel."

I knew that the life had a way of changing your circumstances in a second. The enemy comes to kill, steal, and destroy. Just when you thought he had forgotten about you, the devil always had a way of showing up.

I called my father, Craig because I needed to vent and get some spiritual answers.

I asked, "Daddy, why is God allowing me to go through this? I can't do the schooling thing anymore. I'm quitting tomorrow. I'm tired. The devil is riding my back so hard and Vonte' is out here cutting up. I just can't take anymore."

My Dad listened quietly as I went on to explain how I went to church every Sunday and nobody else at church seemed to be going through what I was. I expressed how tired I was of people telling me to stay prayed up. I *was* praying!

As a preacher, my Father's answers were always short and straight to the point. He asked me what was so special about me that I felt I didn't have to "go through"? He went on to say that Jesus had to.

"Well why does he leave us when the Bible says he will never leave us or forsake us?" I asked anxiously.

My Dad calmly responded and said, "God never leaves us Nicky. It's us that leave him. We go astray and try to handle things on our own. Just because you are going through some things, it doesn't mean he's left you."

He went on to tell me to go home and listen to the words from Michael Jackson's song and envision God saying those very words to me. He said although it seemed like God was far away, he was right there going through it all with me.

My Dad lifted my spirit when he told me that he wasn't worried about me quitting school.

"You ain't never been a quitter Nicky," he said, "Now get a good night's sleep and call me tomorrow."

I wanted so badly to be mad at my Dad. I expected him to say or do a lot more regarding the situation, but when I went home that night, I realized that the information he gave me may have seemed small, but it allowed me to look at things from a different perspective.

I listened to Michael Jackson's song that evening before going to bed and I woke up the next morning feeling like I could conquer the world. I was ready for anything life had to throw my way.

Chapter Twenty-Seven

I focused on completing the last two classes I needed to graduate. As I prepared for graduation, I continuously prayed over my son. I knew that I needed God to step in and take control of the situation.

I learned that when God is blessing you, the devil comes in to start confusion to take your mind off your blessing or to create doubt in you and make you feel that you aren't even worthy to be blessed.

God said that "we are more than conquerors" and I knew that I could do all things through Christ who strengthened me.

Vonte' got into a little trouble and wound up in jail. I thank God that he figured out quickly that being in jail was not what he wanted. It took jail time to make a believer out of him.

When he got out, he enrolled in college and leave the street life behind.

I knocked out my last two classes and graduation day had come. My mother had planned a party and had gotten everything in order.

I was so happy! I did it! It was a long road but I was graduating with a Bachelor's degree in Social and Criminal Justice! Four years on the education roller coaster had come to an end!

In the meantime, my youngest son had started living the street lifestyle. I figured at first that it was just a phase and he would grow out of it, but he started becoming comfortable in the lifestyle.

I told God that I knew he wasn't about to let me go through this again. I went through some things with Cree and Vonte' but they were relatively minor. Sammie was taking the cake! Why would my baby raise so much hell right now?

I cried out to God. I told him I was just trying to make it like everybody else. I knew that the devil must be mad all over again because he couldn't get me to quit, now he was attacking my baby boy.

Every time I looked around, Sammie was in juvenile with a major charge. I remember one day talking to God and saying, "God, I know I did some crazy things in my past and some of the things I did, my own child is now facing. I need you to intervene on this one!'

When I lived the lifestyle my son was now living, I didn't get caught, but my son was now facing some serious charges.

It's crazy how things come back full circle to haunt you.

My son was facing five counts of Aggravated Assault, one count of Aggravated Robbery, one count of Retaliation, and Possession of a Firearm.

Although he had been charged with those crimes I knew he wasn't guilty of them all. We went back and forth to court with him and kept praying that God would show him mercy and keep his hand on him. And he did.

I hit my knees and cried out to God, "I changed my life around. I moved to a better neighborhood, went back to school and have done my very best! I go to church on Sundays and mid-week Bible study! What is it that you want from me God?"

Four of the Aggravated Assault charges were dropped, the Possession of a Firearm was dismissed, and he was placed on probation for the remaining.

By now I had met and married a man they call "LX". He not only took on the role as my husband, he took on the role of a father. He also tried getting through to Sammie.

It was so attractive to me when a man not only accepted you, but accepted you and your children as a full package.

"LX" let me know that my struggles were his struggles and although he would allow me to work things out with my children, he would jump in to help whenever I needed him.

This husband of mine had proven to me that I would never have to face obstacles alone. My fights were his fights, my children were his children, my joys were his joys, and my mother was his mother.

One night, I was braiding his hair when the phone rang. I see from the caller ID that it's Sammie, so I answer with my usual greeting for him, "What up little dude?"

A different voice responded, "Ms. Robinson, this is detective Johnson with the Austin Police Department and we need you to come to the hospital go give permission for Sammie to be treated."

My heart began racing. I screamed into the phone, "What's wrong with my son?"

The Detective answered immediately, "He's been shot."

I grabbed shoes, keys, and was running out the door with "LX" right behind me. I began asking the detective a million questions trying to find out where my son was shot and how badly was he hurt.

The police officer didn't have a lot of information but because Sammie was still considered a minor, they hospital couldn't treat him without parental consent. I was also told to bring another pair of clothing for him because his clothing was soaked with blood.

I drove to the hospital at speeds over 100 miles per hour trying not to break down. When I arrived at the hospital two detectives approached me and asked was I Samuel's mother? I told them that I was and then they asked if I brought more clothing. I told them that I hadn't but that my daughter was on the way with some.

I rushed through the doors and saw a trail of blood that led from the entrance to the back. There was even a bloody handprint on the rail. That was when I broke down.

Was this my son's blood? What happened? Lord, I couldn't take this!

I walked up to the nurse's station and she slid the window back and asked if I had Sammie's insurance card and his asthma inhaler.

 I handed her his insurance card and told her I would call and have his sister bring his inhaler. I wanted to see my son and I began crying harder.

She told me that she knew that I was worried and if it were her son, she'd be worried as well but she assured me that he would be ok and that the bullet wound was not life-threatening.

I found out that he'd been shot in his right arm. The bullet entered through the front of his arm and exited through the back. She continued to tell me that he just needed a few stitches and he should be good.

I appreciated the information. From mother to mother, she knew that I was hurting.

Chapter Twenty-Eight

After we made it through Sammie's shooting incident, I began to pray that God would turn his life around.

I learned that we must be careful of the things we expose our children to. I thought about my past and everything that I'd went through.

Although I tried to keep my children from harm's way, it still wasn't enough. They don't even have to be in a bad neighborhood to become products of their environment. They can simply hang around the wrong friends at school.

Even being in a perfect situation does not mean your children won't travel down the wrong path. My daughter Cree used to love to pull up to people's houses and fight.

One day I was getting on her case about doing that when she told me, "Mama, remember when you used to fight a lot? You never let anyone call you out without handling it."

I tried to explain to her that I had come a long way since then. I told her that today, I let people slide because I realize how much I have to lose and I want better for my life.

I let things fly over my head now because I realize that I have people watching. My children and my grandchildren.

Sammie once told me that he knew he was destined to go to jail and live the lifestyle on the streets, because look who his dad was. That statement alone hurt me.

I told him that even though that was his daddy's way of life, I reminded him of what I'd overcome.

The Bible says in Proverbs 22:6 "Train up a child in the way he should go and when he is old, he will not depart from it." So, if he wanted to use his parent as an example, why not use the one who was in his life from the start. Me.

Day in and out, I made sure my children had everything they needed and most the things they wanted. I was the one who tried to keep my family grounded and together, keeping us in church and learning about God. No matter what came my way, I was the one who pushed through the barriers and overcame all the obstacles so that I could show my children that no matter how old you are or where you are in life, it's never too late to go after your dreams.

Yes. Why not look at the parent that tried her best to show you that with God's help, you can do whatever you set your mind to. You could create the life you wanted and that your past doesn't have to dictate your future. The things from your past can be used as lessons to propel you on your journey. Embrace everything you've been through because God may have needed you to go through those things to get where you are headed.

Sammie decided to get back in school and tried to put the things from his past behind him. I continued to pray that God would continue to bless my marriage, my children, my bonus children, my grandchildren, and my parents.

Sammie's teacher told me of a program that he could take and graduate a year early. He had mostly all of his credits and she believed he was a good candidate for the program because overall, he was a great student.

The teacher told me all the requirements to get into the program, but explained that there was a $250 fee for the final test.

I had a talk with Sammie later that night. I told him that I knew he could pass the test on the first try and asked him would he do this, not just for me; but for himself.

There was nothing that could hold Sammie from success if he wanted it. He wasn't stupid, by far, and was a loving, kind person. Mostly, he was MINE. He was the kid who came into my bedroom to make sure he told me goodnight. He was the child that called out of the clear blue sky just to check on his mama.

I told Sammie all the benefits of graduating a year early and especially letting him know that he could get a job and make his own money. I told him that he could go to college and have a better chance at life.

He went in and took the test and told me that he passed it on the first try and would be graduating in June.

My heart was happy. I would have three high school graduates. For a mother who had been a single parent for most of her children's life, who had once been in a gang and sold drugs, this was a huge accomplishment.

I was grateful that my mother never gave up on me. That taught me how to never give up on my children.

Now, I have three high school graduates. Some going to college, some working and taking care of their family.

I'm still working hard and using all my God given talent for writing, knowing that no matter what we go through as a family, we'll come through it together.

There is still much work that needs to be done but one thing for sure, we know that we are a family. And family is worth fighting for.

BENDABLE BUT UNBREAKABLE

.

Author, Arnikia Robinson was born Ft. Lauderdale, Florida and raised in Texas. She is an author, poet, entrepreneur, and a singer/songwriter with multiple college degrees. A mother of three children and two grandchildren. Her biggest influence and inspiration is her Aunt, Author Lille R. Charles.

Arnikia published her first book of poetry "Experiences with Love" in 2013 and is now back with her powerful memoir "Bendable BUT Unbreakable" in which she shares her life experiences as a troubled teen who found her way and now uses her story to help others.

As a teenager, she learned that the only way to have things was to go out and get it, as a woman she still grinds but knows that the only way to get it is with the help of God.

She hopes that this EXPLOSIVE book will INSPIRE some and EMPOWER others as she uses her gift of writing to let you know, "You may be bendABLE but you are unbreakABLE…because GOD is ABLE."

Made in the USA
Monee, IL
03 September 2020